To Olly

With much love & best wishes,
wishing many happy extractions for the future,
keep on reading!

Graham J. Burton Smith

xxx.

IV / 1982

Behind the scenes of

Gymnastics

Behind the scenes of

Gymnastics

Graham Buxton Smither

Photography by
Alan E Burrows
with Graham Buxton Smither

PROTEUS
London & New York

Among the many people who have inspired, conspired, and perspired in the realization of this book, the author wishes to give special thanks to Romek Richardson, Nik Stuart, Nicolae Vieru, Mili Simionescu, Nadia, Gheorghe Gorgoi, Anca, Christina, and above all, for her inexhaustible patience and extreme tolerance, Liisa.

PROTEUS BOOKS is an imprint of
The Proteus Publishing Group

United States
PROTEUS PUBLISHING COMPANY, INC.
747 Third Avenue, 14th Floor
New York, N.Y. 10017
distributed to the trade by:
CHARLES SCRIBNER'S SONS
597 Fifth Avenue
New York, N.Y. 10017

United Kingdom
PROTEUS (PUBLISHING) LIMITED
Bremar House,
Sale Place,
London, W2 1PT.

ISBN 0 906071 36 4 — UK
      0 906071 61 5 — US

First published in US October 1980
First published in UK September 1980
Designed and typeset by
DP Press, Sevenoaks, England.

Printed and bound in Italy by
Inter-World Publishing Enterprises.

Contents

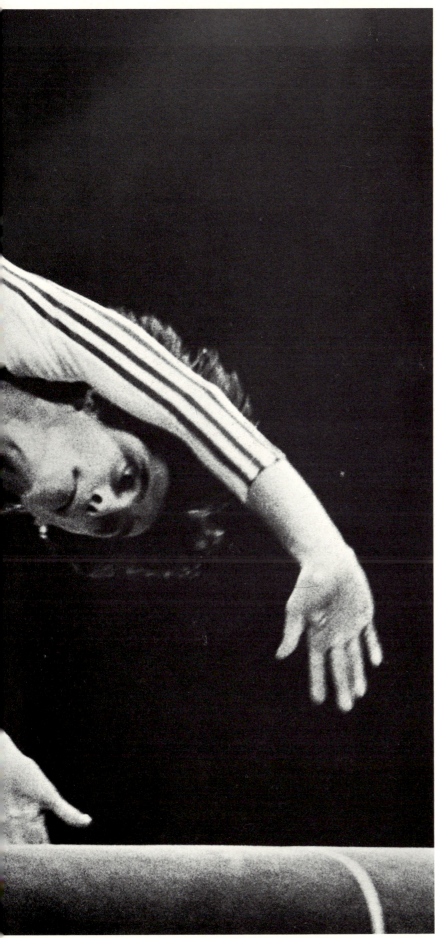

Foreword

Gymnastics has seen a remarkable advance in its standards during the last few years and it is difficult to keep pace with all the new ideas in it. If it is hard for us as gymnasts or coaches, it must be much worse for the spectators and supporters to try to stay abreast of all the developments.

When you watch a competition, all you are seeing is the 'tip of the iceberg', for it represents years of dedication and hard work by many, many people who never get to enter the Competition Arena. To really appreciate the performances in the major events, you should try to understand some of the behind-the-scenes work that has gone into them.

I have been fortunate to have excellent support from my family and the Romanian Gymnastics Federation to enable me to participate, enjoy and succeed in my chosen sport. The successes that my country has enjoyed recently have been the result of team-work coupled with an advanced and enlightened coaching system. In the modern, competitive sport, this is the only way to ensure progress and success.

Gymnastics had dominated my life and like all sports people, I have had bad moments as well as great triumphs and it is important that you learn from them and try to overcome them. It is a sport that brings out many of the best qualities in us, like respect, self-discipline, tolerance, and the ability to work as part of a team, not just for personal achievement.

I am delighted to be asked to write the foreword to this book, for I know that the author is showing the sport in all its aspects. All of us involved in gymnastics know that there are problem areas and that these must be faced. It is a good thing that some people are prepared to examine them and place them into a true perspective. There is much more that is good in the sport than is bad, and I wish everyone continued enjoyment of it.

Nadia Comăneci

Continental

1 The World of Gymnastics

Of all the sports, none expresses the beauty of the human form as perfectly as gymnastics. The word comes from the Greek 'gymnos', meaning naked, and was a reference to the state in which athletes competed in the arenas, unencumbered by clothing. However, you must go back a lot further than the time of the Greek Empires in order to discover the first references to a sport which can be related to contemporary gymnastics. It even pre-dates the Egyptian civilisations because the Sumerians are known to have used elements of gymnastics both in the dance associated with religious ceremony or story telling and also in the training exercises of the King's Bodyguard.

Gymnastics as an identifiable sport really began in Germany in the latter part of the 18th century, thanks largely to the efforts of Friedrich Jahn, often described as the founder of modern gymnastics. He is generally acknowledged with the introduction of the parallel bars, high bar, pommelled horse, and balance beam into the sport. His approach centered around the development of muscular power in order to execute complex and dynamic moves in association with the apparatus which he had helped to develop. However, he did not have it entirely his own way, for one of his contemporaries, a Swede called Pehr Ling, had instituted a system diametrically opposed to Jahn's philosophy. He favored a more expressive form of gymnastics, placing a greater degree of emphasis on flowing movement such as may be seen in the floor exercise, and was greatly alarmed by the immense physical demands and risks inherent in Jahn's practices.

The two different approaches led to a deep division in the world of this developing sport. Was gymnastics truly a sport or merely a form of physical education? This debate still goes on today though in a much moderated form. Gymnastics really received international recognition when in 1896 it was admitted to the Olympic Games, but originally only men were allowed to participate. It was not until 1928 that women were able to compete, and for that enlightened move we must all be very grateful. Where would the renaissance in the sport be, but for the immense popularity of the women's events?

The real breakthrough for the modern sport occurred as a result of a complete accident at the 1972 Munich Olympic Games in the program scheduling for the international television transmission. There was an unfilled gap in the airtime, none of the major events were taking place and fortuitously, cameras were in the gymnastics hall capturing the mesmeric performance of an elfin Russian girl called Olga Korbut. The producer decided to transmit those pictures and, as a result, Olga and gymnastics became 'an overnight sensation'.

It is hardly surprising that this brief coverage led to such an increase in the popularity of the sport, for few sports lend themselves so perfectly to translation to the small screen. An event which involves the human form in disciplined flowing or dynamic movements is always exhilarating to watch, especially when it takes place in a competitive atmosphere. Most spectators at a major competition are not specialists and enjoy an overall impression of the routines

The delightful Olga at the European Championships in Wembley, 1973.

of the participants. This is enough to whet most people's appetites for the sport, but it also means that many of the delicate and most fascinating nuances of the moves are not fully appreciated and often you can hear people asking each other: 'How on earth do they do that? I wish I could see it again.' The problem is that the exercises in gymnastics are now so technically complex and often executed at such speed that the move is completed before its full impact has registered on the audience. Here the small screen comes to the rescue of the arm-chair fan, allowing as it does the invaluable benefit of a replay and also a slow-motion display. Although many sports benefit from the versatility of a televised transmission, gymnastics is arguably the one that needs it the most. Ice-skating is becoming more like a form of ice-gymnastics and it too shares the same problems of complexity and speed of movement. Without the coverage on television, you would not be enjoying the incredible advances in the sport of gymnastics, but equally, the massive intrusion of international broadcasting has given rise to new problems and priorities in its management. These areas will be dealt with in detail later in the book but for now, suffice to say that when money, politics, and personality begin to take precedence over the ethos of the sport, the future looks very

Under the cold stare of the television camera, Irina Derjugina performs with the superb artistry we have come to expect of her. Her superb good looks gave her the opportunity of a film career, but she refused it in favor of gymnastics.

bleak for the purists. The governing body of the sport which has to deal with those problems as well as the technical ones associated with setting competitive and judging standards is the International Gymnastics Federation based in Switzerland.

Gymnastics is divided into several different and distinct disciplines, the most widely recognized being that of Artistic Gymnastics, which is the event one always associates with the Olympic Games. The other forms are Modern Rhythmic Gymnastics, Sports Acrobatics and Tumbling and these are all gaining in popularity.

Modern Rhythmic Gymnastics is exclusively for women to participate in and is based on the floor work in Artistic Gymnastics, but has an additional dimension to it which requires new skills of the competitor. Hand apparatus has been added to the floor exercise, and where this is executed without any apparatus, the requirements for the elements in the routine are different from those in Artistic Gymnastics. The floor exercise without apparatus is far more balletic than its Artistic counterpart and no form of tumbling is permitted. Emphasis is placed on flowing movement in close harmony with the musical accompaniment. You will see a closer link between the gymnast's body movements and the music through the choreography than is the case in Artistic routines. Grace, poise, and suppleness are the prerequisites of this discipline in order to demonstrate adequately the leaps, scales, body waves, steps and pirouettes that are such a feature of this most beautiful exercise.

There are five pieces of hand apparatus used, namely clubs, a rope, hoop, ball, and a ribbon. They must be used as if they were an extension of the performer's body and must therefore harmonize with the rhythm of her body movement and expression. The apparatus may never be static and obviously each has its own variety and style of movements which require special skills of the gymnast and are carefully monitored by the judges in a competition.

The clubs are always used as a pair and are 40 to 50 centimeters long and weigh 150 grams each. They may be used independently so that, for example, one may be thrown while the other is twirled by the wrist of the alternate hand. They may be used to beat out a rhythm to reinforce the dynamics of the routine, or they may be circled or swung with the arms extended.

The rope is exactly that — nothing but a length of rope, without handles. There is no standard length for the rope because it varies according to the height of the gymnast. It may be swung, thrown or indeed swung so as to curl around the contours of the gymnast's body. When it is used for skipping, the judges are looking for more advanced forms of the basic move.

The hoop presents yet another challenge to the competitor. At senior level its internal diameter must be within the limits of

The clubs are here being used as extensions of the arms by Natalia Krascheninnikova.

11

Irina Derjugina, whose fiery temperament and expressiveness helped her to become the World Individual Overall Champion in London, 1979.

80 to 90 centimeters. It can be rolled, thrown, rotated, swung or turned. The gymnast may also pass through it, or indeed jump over it provided that it is still in motion. Once again, all the movements with the apparatus must be fluent and in harmony with her body.

The ball makes great demands of the competitor because she may not hold it at any stage of the exercise, though it may be balanced in the palm during circling or swinging arm movements. It may be rolled either over the gymnast's body or along the floor, and of course, it may be thrown-to-catch or bounce-and-catch. If the performer wishes to bounce it directly, this must be executed as a part of a complete body movement using a flexible wrist. This is rather different from the more familiar form of bouncing technique used in basketball.

The final piece of apparatus is the ribbon, arguably the most exciting and beautiful for the spectator to watch. It has a length of 6 meters and is between four and six centimeters in width. It is attached to a stick of 50 to 60 centimeters in length by means of a form of swivel mechanism that permits unrestricted movement of the length of material. The ribbon should be made of satin or a synthetic material having similar properties. As with all the other pieces of apparatus, there are several different movements that are expected by the judges. Circles and swings are executed with the arm fully extended and the ribbon must transcribe a perfect curve. When a snaking pattern is used, this pattern must extend along the full length of the material; similarly so with the concentric circles created in a spiral movement. The combination of a stride or split leap with a figure-of-eight from the ribbon is the sort of stunning visual image that can be created with this

One of the many fine gymnasts in the USA, exhibiting superb tension on the rings.

Galina Shugurova, former World Champion from the Soviet Union, at the end of another winning performance with the hoop.

exhilarating discipline. Throws are permitted, but the ascent and descent characteristics of the ribbon are the least predictable aspect of all the pieces of apparatus, and maintaining a symmetry of shape in the ribbon is extremely difficult.

All the apparatus in Modern Rhythmic Gymnastics may be performed either as a solo or a group exercise, the group consisting of six competitors. Choreography is of paramount importance in this form of gymnastics, emphasizing as it must the primary qualities of elegance, suppleness, amplitude, extension, expressiveness, and harmony between music, gymnast and apparatus. It is without doubt one of the most spectacular versions of the sport.

Sports Acrobatics, which encompasses Tumbling, is the last form of competitive gymnastics familiar to spectators. Although its origins go back at least to Sumerian times, the contemporary version of this sport is only now beginning to gain a universal interest. Unlike the two previous forms of gymnastic sports already mentioned, this is not governed by the International Gymnastics Federation (FIG). The governing body concerned here is the International Federation of Sports Acrobatics (IFSA) which was formed only as recently as 1973. The first World Championships were held in Moscow in 1974 and proved a considerable success.

The only pieces of apparatus required for

The harmony of man
and woman expressed
through the mixed pairs
in Sports Acrobatics.
The exponents here are
Vadim Pismenny and
Irina Zagorui.

this type of gymnastics are a tumbling strip of 25 meters in length and 1½ meters in width, and the same gymnastic floor mat of 12 meters square that is used in both Artistic and Modern Rhythmic Gymnastics.

There are seven events to be competed for in Sports Acrobatics. They are men's acrobatic jumps, women's acrobatic jumps, men's pairs, women's pairs, mixed pairs, men's groups, and women's trios. The first two events are the Tumbling routines and are the most dynamic and exciting to watch. Each performer may execute two runs which each contain different required elements. The first must contain three somersaults but no twists of 180 degrees or greater. The second must include several of these twists, and generally, both runs will finish with some explosive form of somersault. The quadruple back somersault is the current goal that the men are striving for, and the women are not far behind. It is unlikely, however, that women will reach quite this milestone, assuming no illegal drug-assistance, because of the type of muscle fiber that the female body contains. It is not as conducive to an explosive movement as is the fiber in a man's muscles.

In the remaining five events, all performed on the floor mat, for both the compulsory and the voluntary exercises, two routines must be performed. In the first, the judges are looking for strength, support and balance work, and in the second, they are looking for amplitude and fluent, harmonious movement.

The pairs' exercises are very easy on the eye; it is usual for one of the gymnasts to be more powerful and to specialize in the lifting, throwing, and support work, while the lighter of the two will concentrate on the balance work. How many of us that witnessed it will ever forget the first time we saw Vladimir Nazarov and Vladimir Alimanov demonstrating their one-armed handstand on the head of the partner (Nazarov) who was in a full planche on the mat? The mixed pairs shows the contrast of the two physiques and the two styles of the competitors most strikingly. Of all the forms of gymnastics, the mixed pairs in Sports Acrobatics exemplifies most beautifully the great difference, yet most perfect harmony, between the male and female body.

The men's group event involves four gymnasts performing as a team. For the first part of their routine they have to construct a human pyramid, followed by a sequence concentrating on synchronized movement, somersaults and throws. Needless to say, the pyramids are a most impressive display of strength, but spare a thought for the poor man at the base who has to support all his teammates!

The women's trio perform to much the same requirements as the men's group, though a greater emphasis is placed on their interpretation of the accompanying music, and therefore the choreography is of considerable importance. Their greater suppleness is used to add a delicacy to the construction of the pyramid, and enhance the elegance and rhythm of the second routine.

Because neither Sports Acrobatics nor Modern Rhythmic Gymnastics are as popular or as widely recognized as Artistic Gymnastics, this book will devote most of its pages to the latter. Many of the general points that will be raised when we go 'behind the scenes' will apply to all the forms of gymnastics mentioned and we will not consider the less popular variations of the sport in closer detail, except where an important point hinges on the difference between the different forms of gymnastics.

One kind of gymnastics that has not yet been mentioned is educational gymnastics. This term refers to the formal style of physical education practiced in schools, colleges, and often nowadays, in factories and offices. It has no real competitive aim but is merely designed to make people take some form of controlled exercise. The role and importance of educational gymnastics varies considerably in different parts of the world. In much of the Western world, for example, it is often treated as a tedious imposition and generates less than enthusiastic participation accordingly! In the Far East or in Eastern Europe it is considered a daily essential to maintain alertness and general health — especially good for educational or industrial productivity. In the more affluent and industrial nations, most people lead a sedentary life and have only recently started becoming aware of the risks to their health that it poses. In the more liberal societies, there is an inbuilt resistance to seeking exercise through the very formal regime that seems to be the hallmark of educational gymnastics.

Before we penetrate the whole system involved in the development, organization and running of the gymnastics world, we should take a closer look at just what Artistic Gymnastics involve.

Boris Shakhlin locked in his own private battle with the horse.

2 Competition

One of the first things that one notices when looking inside a training or competition hall for the first time is the array of bizarre pieces of equipment standing, lying or hanging around, all of which seems carefully designed to torture the human body. Difficult to believe though it may be, none of these pieces of apparatus was designed by the Inquisition — despite the comments of some of the less fortunate competitors to that effect!

The reliance on a large amount of apparatus is one of the most distinctive features of Artistic Gymnastics, and has been so ever since the acceptance, albeit grudgingly in some circles, of Jahn's philosophy and approach to the sport. Each of the pieces of apparatus, or 'disciplines' as they are referred to, is designed to extract different skills from the gymnast and hopefully, to allow them to be demonstrated most effectively. Men must compete over six disciplines, but women only have four. Only two disciplines are common to both men's and women's exercises: the floor and the vault. In the vault, however, the men vault along the horse and the women vault across it.

In order of competition, the six disciplines for men are: floor exercises, pommelled horse, rings, vaulting horse, parallel bars, and high (horizontal) bar. For women the four disciplines are vaulting horse, asymmetric (uneven) bars, balance beam, and floor exercises. Let us now take a closer look at each of these disciplines, starting with the men's apparatus.

The floor exercise takes place in a 12 meter square area of specially constructed matting. It is made up of a number of panels which have a rubber base and laminates of plywood, on top of which is laid the carpet. The combination of the rubber base and foam layers between the plywood gives the carpeted area both a degree of springiness and also a shock-absorbent quality. These are essential characteristics in view of the immense pounding that the floor area must take during both training and competition. There is a one meter wide border around this square and at no stage during an exercise must any part of the gymnast's body come into contact with it. Every time this border is crossed, a deduction of 0.10 is made from the final score, which is a possible maximum of 10.00 points. At the highest level of competition, this could represent the difference between a gold medal and a bronze.

The duration of the exercise is between 50 and 70 seconds and in fact the competitor will receive an audible indicator at those precise moments. The exercise must be fluent and must form a complete and harmonious entity. The most dynamic parts of this routine are to be found in the tumbling sequences and in the leaps. These are all areas where the agility of the gymnast is tested to the full. In addition, he must demonstrate strength and balance moves, typified by various forms of handstands and scales. Handstands will generally be pressed, which means that the body and legs will be powered up by sheer muscular effort rather than by control of the momentum resulting from a kick or swing. To watch someone like the Russian 1979 World Champion, Alexandre Detiatin, executing

That great Jugoslavian competitor, Miroslav Cerar, demonstrating the sort of form that helped to re-awaken interest in the pommelled horse.

19

a planche with split legs, on fingertips, and then slowly raising body and legs into a perfect handstand is a truly astounding experience. A scale is a form of one-legged balance in which the trunk and the free leg are extended along various planes, and the one demonstrated by the competitor must be held without any wavering for a few seconds.

The gymnast is required to utilize the whole floor area during the exercise and failure to do so will be reflected in the judging. For the tumbling sequences, he needs the benefit of the 16.97 meters diagonal length to ensure the display of enough superior difficulties and also variety. However, a long run-up for the sequence will be penalized, so speed and agility are of the essence. In recent years, male gymnasts have started to give more thought to the choreography linking the different elements of the routine. The standard of men's floor exercises is improving by leaps and bounds (it's difficult to resist the occasional pun) but there is still quite some room for progress towards elusive perfection.

The pommelled horse, sometimes referred to as the side horse, is all too often the graveyard of gymnastic ambition. It is the most mentally and physically constraining and demanding of all the disciplines and following, as it does, the free expression of the floor work is hardly easy on the gymnast.

The horse is the same length as the vaulting horse at 1.60 meters and the height is maintained at 1.10 meters. Unlike its vaulting twin, it has two handles across the central part of its body, these being the pommels. The horse is divided into three supposed sections, those being the croup, the saddle (the area contained by the pommels), and the neck. The gymnast must travel and work on all three sections, and throughout the entire exercise the only parts of his body which may come into contact with the horse are his hands. No stops or pauses are permitted and his work must be executed at a constant pace. All movements of the body and the legs are swung, ideally from the shoulders. Strength and balance are essential for this discipline, as are perfect body tension and total concentration. Strong shoulders and long arms are hardly a hinderance either! All the top exponents of the pommelled horse keep their chests over an imaginary center line along the back of it, whether working from a front support, rear support or whatever. There are certain

prescribed movements on this apparatus such as forward and reverse scissors; double leg circles are a popular movement as are the most dramatic flairs, named after their innovator, the American gymnast Kurt Thomas. For many years the Hungarian, Zoltan Magyar, has reigned supreme in this discipline but now innovators from America, China and Russia are widening the area of competition.

The next instrument of torture on the agenda are the rings; these too require great shoulder strength, but the mechanics are very different from those of the pommelled horse. The two rings each have an internal diameter of some 18 centimeters and hang from straps attached to wire cables which are in turn attached to the main frame in such a way as to allow the rings to be 2.5 meters from the ground. The distance between the rings is 45 centimeters.

Power-to-weight ratio, body tension,

Sergei Diamidov in a superb crucifix at the 1965 European Championships in Antwerp.

Vladimir Markelov using his great strength in a finger-tip balance during his floor exercise.

20

flexibility, balance, and an understanding of body mechanics are all of great assistance on this apparatus. Being blessed with short arms and strong shoulders is almost essential to a top-class competitive exponent. Terms like 'inlocate', 'dislocate', and 'crucifix' reinforce the torturous image that this discipline exudes to both spectator and gymnast. The competitor has to display moves requiring strength, both static and moving, and swings, which are doubly difficult to control because the apparatus is moving at the same time as the gymnast. The rings are supposed to have no motion other than a lateral one, so any rocking back and forth is going to detract from the performance and the final scoring.

Handstands, whether pressed or the result of a controlled swing, are a major feature of a rings exercise, as are various levers. There can be little doubt though, that there are two movements, both strength, which always set the audience buzzing. The first is a full planche which, while it is a strong move on the floor, is positively Herculean on the rings. Balance is more awkward to maintain because of the habit the rings have of moving. The second is the crucifix, a move in which gravity seeks more strongly than usual to destroy the form of the competitor. Here the body must be vertical and the arms completely horizontal and, like all held movements in men's gymnastics, must be maintained for two seconds.

Dismounting from this apparatus is no easy task, again, owing to the mobile nature of the take-off point. However, the top gymnasts defy reason and hospitalization in executing full twisting back somersaults, double back somersaults, and the rest. The search is forever on for new and more difficult dismounts — well, what's a few broken legs between friends?

And for the gymnasts' next trick, ladies and gentlemen — the vaulting horse. This has the virtue of being the quickest piece of apparatus to work on. As pointed out earlier, the men are required to vault along the horse and are not allowed to place their hands on the middle, or saddle, section of it. It is 1.6 meters in length and 1.45 meters high, taller than both the pommelled and the women's horse, the latter two being actually the same height. The maximum length of the run-up permitted is 20 meters for men, whereas for women it is unlimited.

A good run-up is absolutely critical to the correct execution of the vault and most

of the faults that occur can be traced back to this stage of the exercise. Attack and control are the qualities that must be combined with the speed of the gymnast for a run-up that will set him on the right path to a sound vault. Controlled aggression is very much the essence of this exercise. The run-up is similar in nature to that of the long-jumper; it must gather momentum until about the last three paces before take-off when the speed should be constant. One often notices competitors checking their start points meticulously, because for each there is an optimum length of run which they tend to adhere to; consistency here is

most important. The phases of a vault are: run-up – take-off – preflight – push-off – postflight – landing. A useful rule-of-thumb in vaulting is that a low flight onto the horse means a high flight off and vice versa. Because the arms should always be straight when pushing off from the horse, the push must come from the fingers, wrists, and shoulders. On landing, the arms are used to counter the forward momentum of the gymnast, the knees bending in order to allow the legs to act as shock-absorbers. Vaults such as the Yamashita and Tsuka-hara, both named after their Japanese innovators, were until recently considered too demanding for women to perform, but such are the ever-increasing demands of both men's and women's gymnastics that nowadays complex twisting variations must be executed in order to gain a reasonable mark from the judges.

Next, we come to the parallel bars. They are 3.5 meters in length and are variable in both height and width. Care must be taken by the competitor to ensure that this height and separation is adjusted to suit his morphology as carefully as possible. The bars were originally designed by Jahn to help the gymnast develop strength for the pommelled horse. The only parts of the anatomy permitted to come into contact with the apparatus are the arms and hands, and these execute most of the moves in one of three modes: hang, upper arm hang/support, support. Hang refers to any occasion when the shoulders and body are below the level of the hands, and support is the opposite of this. Upper arm hang/support is a reference to those times when the arms, from shoulder to hand, lie along the bars and movements are executed from this position.

Swinging movements dominate the contemporary scene on parallel bars, and the swing to handstand is a key component in any of these exercises. Whether one is watching a backward roll or the masterly Diamidov turn, a static or a swinging move, the complete exercise must have an overall sense of harmony and amplitude to be a success. There is a greater tendency these days to increase the amount of work on just one of the bars and parts of high bar routines are creeping into the parallel repertoire. So too some pommel horse work such as the Thomas flairs. As with the rings, the variety of dismounts available to the gymnast seems to be limitless.

The final piece of men's apparatus is the high bar. This exercise is undoubtedly one of the most impressive of all. The bar is 2.55 meters high and 2.4 meters wide. The performance of the exercise must be dynamic and movement must be continuous. Good body tension and extension are essential to enhance the overall impression of the exercise. It must contain giant circles, support circles, twists, releases to recatch, and changes of grip. This is an exercise which demands a considerable amount of strength of the gymnast, coming as it does, at the end of the whole competition. To get some idea of the immense force acting on the body when swinging fully extended around the high bar, just look at the torque on it. Missing the regrasp after executing a Voronin hop or a Tkachev on this apparatus can be a most painful way of bowing out of world gymnastics. No wonder then that this piece of apparatus is no longer considered suitable for women. The dismounts from the high bar are the most spectacular in all the disciplines of gymnastics, and a full twisting backward somersault from the apparatus is an awesome and exhilarating sight. A double back is now becoming more common. Where will it all end?

We have now taken a very brief look at the six pieces of men's apparatus and can turn our attention to the women and their four disciplines. The first of them utilizes the vaulting horse.

As mentioned earlier, the women's horse is lower than the men's, being 1.10 meters in height, though with the same length of 1.60 meters. The women vault across the saddle of the horse rather than along its back. There is no official limitation to the length of run-up allowed for women, the size of the competition hall being the only governing factor. In both the optional and compulsory exercises the women are allowed two attempts at the vault. These may but need not be identical vaults except in the finals, when they *have* to be different and must also contain turns. All the basic principles that were detailed in the section dealing with the men's vault hold equally well for the women's exercise.

We now arrive at the women's variation on the high bar, known as the asymmetric bars. There are two bars parallel to each other, but one is 2.30 meters and the other 1.50 meters high; the distance between them can be varied to accommodate the differing heights and reaches of the various gymnasts.

The exercise must be fluent, with the emphasis on swinging movements and no held positions are permitted. There must be changes of grip, bars, direction of motion, and alternation between support and hang moves. Turns around both axes, kips, swings to handstand are all moves which the judges are looking for and guarantee a variety of movement throughout this most absorbing discipline. Once again, this discipline has seen incredible advances in technical content and some of the moves rival the daring of the men on the high bar. Anyone who has seen Nadia Comaneci performing her Radochla somersault on the higher bar

Strength and tension are essential to this difficult balance that has become synonymous with Natalia Shaposhnikova's beam routine.

The statuesque and elegant form of Vera Caslavska.

could only marvel at the courage and technical expertise necessary for such an achievement.

Suppleness, agility, strength and courage are prerequisites for this exercise. When watching a polished performance on this apparatus it is an awe-inspiring exercise to reflect on the preparation that has gone into such a presentation — hundreds of hours in training, a lot of time landing unintentionally on the crash mats at the beginning, and a fair number of bruises to prove it all. Fortunately, the bars absorb shock quite effectively if approached in the right manner, so there is no need to wince when a girl beats or wraps on a bar.

It does not matter which bar the gymnast mounts on or dismounts from, but the dismount must be from a swinging move and not a static one. Gymnasts are quite free to mount with the assistance of a springboard if they wish, but the coach has to be snappy in pulling it away or they will strike it painfully with their feet.

The penultimate discipline is that of the balance beam and on this the gymnast looks all too painfully vulnerable. The merest hint of a wobble could be a prelude to disaster and the intake of breath around the auditorium is clearly heard by the competitor. The beam is 5 meters long, 1.20 meters high, and a challenging 10 centimeters wide. Given that the gymnast must display leaps, jumps, pivots, turns, hops, balances, acrobatic elements, and running combinations of steps, this exercise is clearly a recipe for potential disaster. The duration of the exercise is between 1.15 minutes and 1.35 minutes and that is certainly long enough. Grace, poise, agility, balance and fleetness of foot are the hallmarks of a competent beam worker. In fact, many of the elements that

Back in the days when women gymnasts still looked like women rather than prepubescent girls, this elegant Russian teenager, Natasha Kuchinskaya, was proving to be Caslavska's greatest threat. She took the beam gold medal from Vera at the Mexico Olympics in 1968.

At the 1965 Vienna Gymnastrada, Larissa Latynina works under the close and critical eyes of the audience. Because of contemporary security fears, it is rare nowadays to find gymnasts in such close proximity to the spectators at major internationals.

The fiery and rebellious temperament of Shaposhnikova is clearly revealed through the expressiveness of her floor work.

were amazing on the floor only a short while ago are now *de rigeur* for the top competitors on this apparatus. Aerial cartwheels, flic-flacs, standing front and back somersaults, all these can be seen executed at major events. Natalia Shaposhnikova has beguiled the gymnastics fraternity with a one armed balance, girls are working around the beam now and dismounts are becoming more technically complex. Emilia Eberle's perfection of the piked double back dismount is only the start of these superior difficulties. A fine performance on the balance beam lends great stature and authority to a gymnast, but one fall will reduce them to the ranks of mere mortals.

The last of the disciplines is the floor exercise, performed in the same floor area as in the men's exercises. The exercise lasts for anything between 60 and 90 seconds and must contain acrobatic and gymnastic elements and movements, leaps, turns, balances, and body waves like those seen on the beam. There must be at least two tumbling series and nowadays these will almost certainly need to contain a double back somersault or two to merit serious attention. Again, the whole of the floor area must be used and each step outside the border will

cost the gymnast 0.10 points. The connections between the various elements are of great importance and the choreographer plays a major role in this exercise. Musical accompaniment may now be orchestrated, and this must be carefully selected to match the expressiveness, morphology, and temperament of the competitor. The exercise must be rhythmic, dynamic, flowing and must form a harmonious entity, with sufficient variation of connections and elements to avoid dull repetition. This discipline lends itself perfectly to the physical and emotional expressiveness of a woman, and when it is performed in a lively and genuine manner, it is a joy to behold.

Having reviewed all the apparatus involved in Artistic Gymnastics it should be evident that each piece is designed to seek out different qualities that must all be displayed by the modern gymnast. They not only test these qualities, but allow the competitor to demonstrate them in a physically and visually exciting manner. Every range of movement of the human body is expressed and probed by at least one of the disciplines and to master these, and by implication one's own body, is no mean or futile achievement.

3 Gymnastics and the Young

Gymnastics is a young person's sport and this fact is now more apparent than ever, especially when you remember that the world has recently seen the first 14½ year-old triple Olympic champion, the incomparable Nadia Comaneci from Romania. How is it that a sport which is so demanding, mentally and physically, and so technically complex has such a young champion? If Nadia was a 'one-off' this situation could be excused as a freak occurrence, but this age-level is now common among top competitors in women's gymnastics. Because men have a slower rate of physical development, the considerable strength required for their exercises has meant that the early twenties have normally been the years of best performance for their leading gymnasts. However, in the men's events too, the age of the top competitors is lowering into the late teens. How is it that today's children can do so much more with their bodies than most of us ever could and, perhaps more importantly, just what is it doing to them?

When one remembers that most of the finest gymnasts that we marvel at today started on the Olympic gymnastics trail at the age of six, it becomes very important to find out just what sort of role their parents played in their development. In examining this aspect of the sport we find that there is no universally applicable explanation for all parents with children who want to pursue gymnastics competitively. The attitudes of differing societies, schools, parents, governments, and sporting bodies all play their part in determining if and how children may become involved in the sport.

The haunting face and lithe artistry of Shaposhnikova.

Gymnastics is an expressive and artistic sport — that at least is a statement upon which all would agree. What, though, is a sport; in fact, what is sport and what is its purpose? That question is not an excuse to toy with semantics, but demonstrates the widely differing attitudes of society to the pursuits of sport, and in the response lies the key to the chances of a child getting to the top in the highly competitive world of gymnastics. In a society where sporting success is highly prized and given an according priority, a child with the right potential can be reasonably certain of being given every opportunity to achieve it. In societies with a different perspective on sports, any child who has reached the top has done so *despite* the system and, in many cases, is worthy of respect because his or hers is an achievement against far greater odds.

In most liberal Western countries there is a reluctance to involve children in organized, competitive sporting activity at a very early age (though the United States is rapidly becoming an exception for motives very different than those driving Eastern bloc countries). This has been an attitude associated with certain contemporary educational views which advocate a non-disciplinarian, free-expression form of schooling for four to eight-year-olds. It is still a matter of considerable debate as to whether such views have been a good thing; suffice to say that formal educational ideas are taking precedence again. The class-room controversies aside, sport, it can be argued, is a form of personal expression and should be encouraged as such. It has the merits of seeking to encourage individual excellence and also

team responsibility. Although gymnastics is essentially a team sport, the spotlight is always on the individual performer and such a combination is a great builder of self-confidence. Where there have been systems which decried individual ambition and excellence, such as China during the 'cultural revolution', the general level of ability in such areas of sports dropped alarmingly. Achievement motivation is one of the primary drive forces for man's advancement and of course, the young are the key to the future in all fields of endeavor. But where in this scheme of things do parents and children fit and how do they translate their ambitions into reality in gymnastics?

The easiest way of demonstrating how a child can become a gymnast is to take the case of a family in which both the parents and the child are keen to develop his or her interest in the sport, and the child has the innate ability to become a good competitor.

To give ourselves an opportunity to understand the path to the top in the sport, we must be prepared to consider the different systems under which that family unit might live, and therefore, the way these affect the chances for that child to be able to realise his or her full potential. We will consider two obverse systems – the first will be an established Western democracy such as the United States, Great Britain, France, or Sweden; the second will be an Eastern bloc state, Romania being one of the better examples.

Initially, we will assume our budding gymnast to be a six-year-old girl living with her family in a small provincial town. For ease of identification, our Western child will be called Susan and the Eastern child will be called Nadia. To further assist the comparison, Susan is assumed to attend a state-run school rather than a private one.

Susan is becoming frustrated at school because she wants to learn gymnastics but

Group exercises help to instil the team spirit and awareness needed for many of the major competitions.

there are neither the necessary instructors nor the right facilities available to her. On the school curriculum are periodic physical training sessions, which will include primitive elements of gymnastics, but these are informal and involve no form of disciplined exercise. There is one more rigid exercise period per week but this is a very basic form of educational gymnastics which is effectively little more than a keep-fit class. At this point, Susan, with the help of her parents, attempts to overcome the impasse by looking for a gymnastics club to enter. A quick check reveals that the nearest club is in one of the larger towns in their area, say some fifteen miles away. There is a waiting-list for places in it, but Susan is able to get the coach to give her a trial, he recognizes the potential in her and allows her to join the club right away. You may think that at last the problems are over — far from it; it is now that they start to become apparent.

The parents are now faced with several problems. The cost of their daughter's interest begins to loom large in their thoughts. The club fee, clothing, and very possibly additional coaching fees all have to be accommodated. Then there is the round trip to her training of thirty miles; at this stage she is too young to travel unaccompanied. She will have to be driven there and back, which is both a further expense and a very time consuming chore. However, the decision is made to give it a try and Susan is on her way.

What of her East European counterpart? Well, thanks to the Romanian 'Physical Education and Sport Promotion Act' passed in 1967, she has had her interest and capability monitored since kindergarten. In all schools there are daily exercises in educational and compensatory gymnastics as well as both curricular and extra-curricular sports activities. As soon as Nadia's interest and competence in gymnastics is recognized by her teachers, her parents are consulted. It is agreed that she should take a test in the sport before one of the local coaches to see if she really has the potential that they suspect. They agree, as in Susan's case, that she has exceptional talent. Rather than join the local club, it is recommended that she should go to one of the sports schools where the facilities are much better and she is also able to continue studying academic subjects. This will involve the young girl leaving her family to board at the school; her parents are free to visit her during her free time, of course. She can now expect to spend a good four hours a day in the gymnasium during what are the normal schooling periods. This system imposes a minimal financial burden on the parents and avoids monopolizing their spare time in the pursuit of their daughter's sporting activity.

The fluid beauty of the human form in stark contrast with the harsh regularity of the architectural structure. Nadia in her training camp in Bucharest, 1978

If we take up their stories at the age of twelve, we can assess the way their progress is developing. They have both reached the national junior finals and are subsequently admitted to their respective junior international squads. For Susan, this means continuing at her club but also going to training sessions with some of the other girls in the squad under national team coaches. These additional training times are concentrated and allow her access to the apparatus for long periods of time at natural hours of the day. She is now partly subsidized by her Gymnastics Association and this is designed to cover travel to major events and national coaching sessions. Her school curriculum is still preventing her from being able to train at the most suitable hours.

For Nadia, there is little change in the general pattern of life. She remains at the same school, but will by now be training with coaches who are themselves trained to teach a more advanced level of gymnastics. The consistency of her environment is a great benefit to her general stability, and the fact that she is training with other members of the top junior squad all the time is invaluable. It serves to raise her competitive edge and also means that all her training is done at the highest levels of her sport. She can expect to be doing some 24 hours of training in the gymnastics hall each week, and always at the time of day that her body considers conducive to peak performance. Susan will be most fortunate to be able to log the same number of hours and has little chance of choosing their timing. Nadia's cloistered life-style means that there are few external pressures on her that could affect her concentration or dedication to her sporting studies. There is the additional benefit from the coaches' point of view that her eating habits can be carefully controlled in order to help her to get the maximum in performance.

Both girls are now competing internationally, but at this stage their different gymnastics backgrounds are beginning to tell in relation to the technical quality of their exercises. Although both girls started out with exactly the same innate talent, Susan is starting to lag behind in her competition results.

Let us now pick up their trail at the age of sixteen. They are both in their respective senior teams, having passed through the barrier from junior to senior status at the tender age of fourteen. This is a turbulent time for both girls. They have both survived the problems for performance that puberty brings. Susan is faced with a difficult decision concerning whether or not she ought to give up her school studies in order to take a part-time job and be able to spend more time on gymnastics. Academic achievement versus sporting achievement — for Susan it is not an easy choice. Academic examinations rear their ugly heads at this age and it is now that there can often be a conflict between the parents and their child, especially if that child is considered by her teachers as a likely candidate for further education.

For Nadia too, there has been a major change. She has left her last school for the senior women's top school in a different part of the country and under new coaches, in fact under the coaches to the Olympic squad. She has been further removed from her family and finds that generally, she is less able to see people from outside her immediate environment because of her training commitments. This isolation is good for her gymnastics though positively a hinderence to any social life that would otherwise detract from her concentration on sport. Because of the standardization of educational exercises, Nadia is able to continue with her previous academic studies alongside her revised training schedules.

Once again, the standards of the two girls can be seen to be far apart. In the World Championships, where Nadia would expect to finish somewhere within the first ten places overall, Susan finishing in about fortieth position would be considered to have done rather well. Both their achievements and their expectations are a considerable distance apart. But who has really done the best, and which is ultimately the most contented?

It really depends on the relative value put on competitive success versus character development, and also who has had the most difficulties to overcome. Of our two hypothetical examples, there can be little doubt that Nadia has achieved the greater degree of success in her sport, but equally she had all the assistance that she could have wished for from a highly sophisticated sports establishment. It can be argued that Susan's is the greater achievement because she has made enormous progress despite a system that is not geared for her needs in gymnastics. It may well be argued that Nadia will be less able to cope with the everyday problems of working life because she

Youth and experience, gymnast and coach.

has been living in an isolated and specialized community, whereas Susan has had to cope with all the normal pressures of conventional life. Fortunately for Nadia, the Romanian Federation of Gymnastics has more regard for the needs of the individual than some of its East European brethren, like Russia, East Germany and Bulgaria. There the gymnasts are completely isolated from the outside world and at all international events take with them a fearsome number of 'officials' who protect them from the evils of unsanctioned contact with Westerners. This blinkering of their vision helps to ensure that they stay in the field of sports after their competitive careers are ended, because they have experience of little else and will therefore singlemindedly re-invest their experience into the sport as coaches.

Some countries, like West Germany and Japan, have a strong gymnastics heritage. Others, particularly the USA, have a healthy sports-orientated college system, in which those especially adept at sports can receive scholarships to further their pursuit. In fact, the American collegiate attitude to sports is not as helpful to the would-be champion gymnast as it is, say, to the grid-iron footballer or baseball star, because of the extreme youth at which top gymnasts begin their apprenticeship. It remains to be seen whether the boom in interest in women's gymnastics spurred by Olga Korbut's televised magic coupled with the preoccupation of American parents with pushing young sports protegés will produce a consistent medal-winning US team in the years to come.

These countries fall into a kind of midway category, borrowing elements from both the extremes described above, and many consider them to offer an ideal marriage of the principles behind the traditional Western approach and the Iron Curtain philosophy.

Above:
Ballet exercises form an essential part of body preparation for any aspiring gymnast.

Right:
Portrait of the gymnast as a young woman.

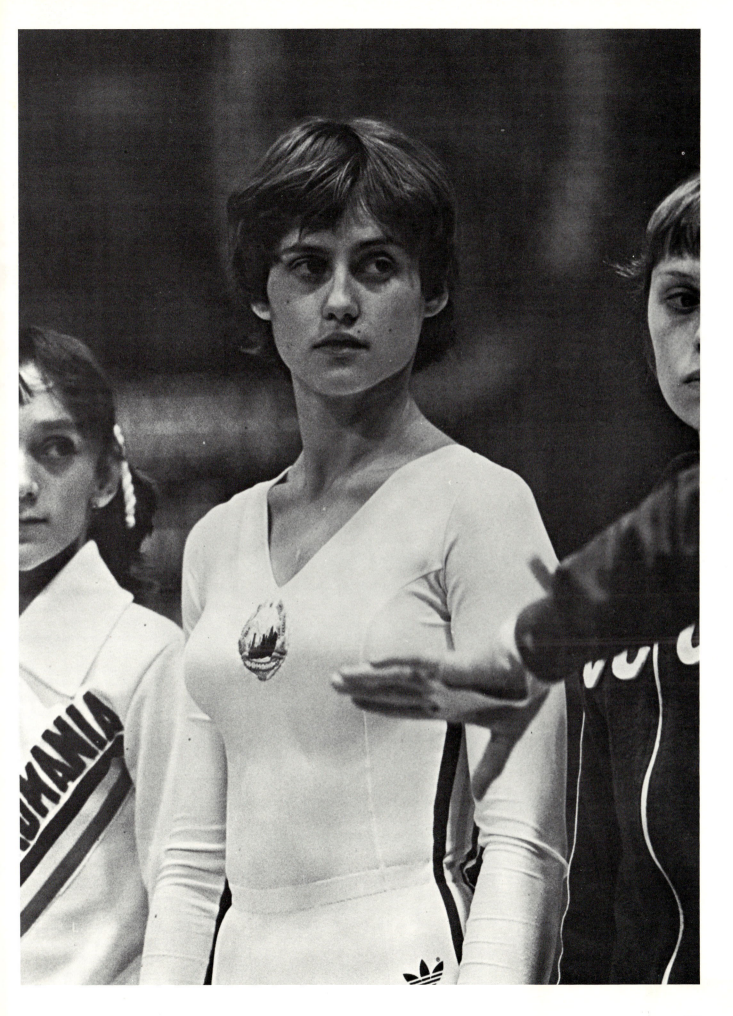

For boys and men the picture is slightly different in that the problems of performance occur at different times from the girls. For the boys the problems start very much earlier. Because strength is needed for nearly all the elements in men's gymnastics, it is very disheartening to the youngsters because, due to the much slower rate of physical development of the male, they find that many of the exercises are impossible for them to perform as well as senior gymnasts. It is here that a gentle blend of persuasion and encouragement on the part of both parents and coaches is vital as a booster to morale. The fact that they can see girls of younger age performing complex routines with greater proficiency is a blow to their confidence and pride. This dismay prompts many promising boys to give up and much potential talent is lost forever. Coaches need to work overtime to instil self-confidence and self-discipline, and force the budding gymnast to persevere with all the boring, repetitive strength-building exercises that are part of the essential groundwork for a successful gymnast. Club participation is a great benefit at this stage because the advantages of a physical regime of work are readily apparent in the senior club competitors who tend to become the peer group. If the boy is able to be taught to enjoy channeling his energies into pure physical effort, the coach is halfway to winning the battle. One major problem concerning those who hope to take up men's gymnastics is simply finding a club with adequate staff and facilities to cope with the men's apparatus. Because of the far greater popularity of women's gymnastics, there are fewer places made available to men. In fact, there are many clubs which devote their efforts solely to women's disciplines. In the West this may well make economic sense, but is hardly conducive to the improvement of the general standards of men's work. The disparity in numbers between the sexes is less obvious in Asia and Eastern Europe because they have a historical tradition of acrobatics which preceded the development of contemporary gymnastics, and in the past most of the performers were men. In the West, the predominance of women has occurred since the media interest generated by Olga Korbut's captivating performances at the Munich Olympic Games. Because Western audiences tend to focus on individual personalities, something actively discouraged in the East, the women have retained their numerical supremacy by virtue of the demand generated by the decision of TV producers that women's gymnastics make more engrossing television; viewing figures seem to bear this out. The greater the media coverage, the greater level of interest, and the stronger the motivation in fledging participants to join the proceedings.

It is the Associations and Federations that administer the sport in the various countries, and they work according to the regulations of the world governing body, the FIG (International Gymnastics Federation). Some of the national bodies are self-financing, but with the enormous demands made on the sport nowadays, this situation is likely to change as the administration and promotion of gymnastics becomes a multi-million dollar industry. Sponsorship by commercial interests is becoming a more and more significant factor in the Profit and Loss Accounts of major tournaments hosted by the West, though it has begun to cause concern on the part of the sport's governing organizations. Commercial sponsorship has led to the disintegration of many amateur sports, the pressures sometimes imposed by sponsors conflicting with the established aims of those sporting authorities. The consequence has often been to split a sport into two, by the creation of a professional variation of the original which tends to cream the finance from the amateur side. This has serious implications for the Olympic movement as well as all popular amateur sports in general.

Once again, this problem does not arise in societies in which the state considers sport to be an integral part of its scheme of things and finances it accordingly. It is simply appended to the general educational system and so deems itself to be non-professional. One of the most important tasks of Western gymnastics organizations is to ensure that the sponsorship is given directly to themselves and that nothing is filtered en route. This being done, they maintain their amateur status, but if any individual competitor was to promote, directly or indirectly, knowingly or unknowingly, a service or product in connection with their gymnastics, they would lose their amateur status with little chance of appeal.

Most national associations are in receipt of some form of state subsidy in addition to their membership income, the proceeds of the marketing of their own literature

and equipment, and the returns from the promotion of displays and competitions. A professional gymnastics circuit will have been launched by the time you read this book, and this does seem to be a worrying pointer to the future — purists beware!

From the moment a parent enrols a child in a club and the national gymnastics authority, a complex train of circumstances will gradually unfold which hopefully will result in the child participating proudly and happily in his or her chosen sport. Assistance rather than interference is required of the parents in all cases. A parent should have no more access to a training session in a gymnastics hall than would be given by a school to attend a child's classes. In training, the coach must receive all the trust, respect, and obedience that a parent would normally command — in fact, the coach must subvert the authority of the parents during his

or her sessions.

The club must provide the framework for the child's sporting development and nurture a healthy competitive instinct. The school should be aware of the importance to the character-forming of a child that the pursuit of his or her gymnastics interest can have. It should attempt to be flexible when there are serious clashes between the academic and the sporting calendar. The association or federation should provide every assistance in all phases of the gymnast's sporting life. If it looks after its members, they will move heaven and earth to reciprocate. However, as we have seen, there are wide differences between the way many countries perceive the role of sports and their importance to society, and these differences profoundly influence the extent to which the sports in question are able to prosper.

The constant intrusion by the attendant press corps can prove a great destructive influence on a young person. Nadia's complete disregard for the blandishments and criticisms of the press have left her unaffected by them.

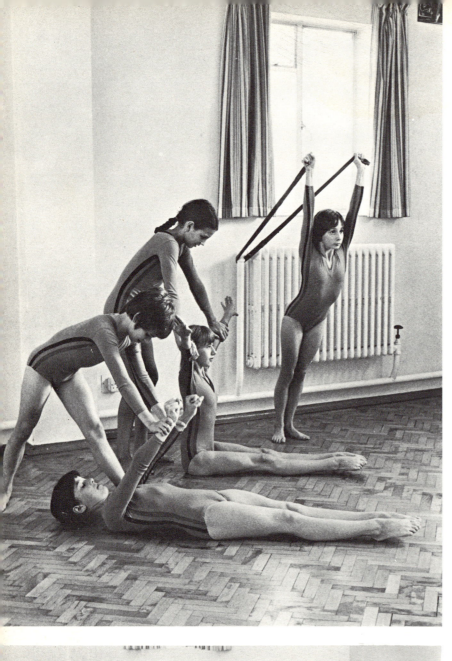

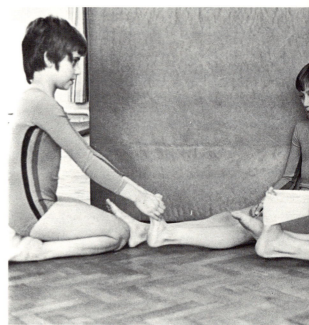

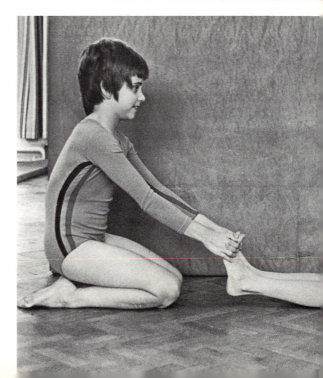

All of these conditioning exercises, being demonstrated by girls from the Hillingdon Club in England, are basic to the development of suppleness and strength and could, in fact, benefit most people. For, as can be seen, there is no real need for any complex equipment in order to be able to do them.

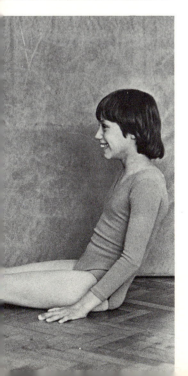

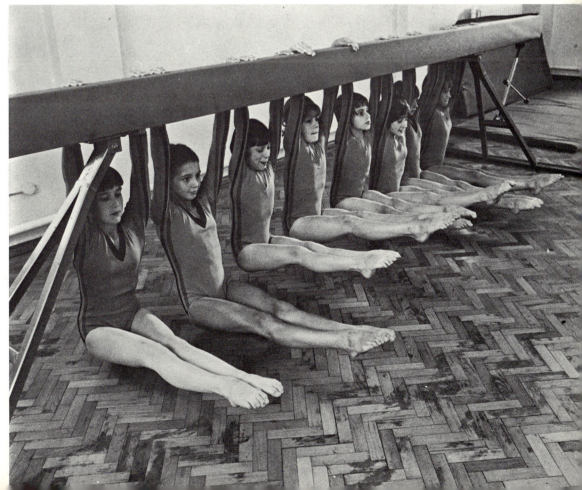

4 Winners

It must be obvious to even the most casual observer that there are certain countries that tend to dominate the gymnastics scene. Some of the reasons for their continued success are obvious, others less so, and we will now take a 'behind-the-scenes' look at the countries concerned.

It is an incredible achievement that, since women started competing on the contemporary apparatus during the Helsinki Olympic Games of 1952, the Soviet Union has won every Olympic Women's Team Title. In the men's events, over the same period, Japan and the Soviet Union have shared the Team Title, with Japan having had the edge until recently. Czechoslovakia, East Germany, Hungary, and latterly, Romania have all been contenders for team silver or bronze medals at the highest levels of competition. The USA and China have at last been able to fulfil their promise internationally, and we can expect to see Cuba and Korea becoming innovators alongside of them.

Of all the countries, none has consistently dominated the international gymnastics scene as much as the Soviet Union. It has a well of talent of seemingly infinite capacity and new stars are forever forcing their way to the top. Just contemplate some of the illustrious names in the recent history of the sport: Latynina, Astakhova, Kuchinskaya, Lazakovitch, Turischeva, Korbut, Kim, Mukhina, Shaposhnikova; Titov, Shakhlin, Azarian, Voronin, Andrianov, Detiatin, Tkachev, Deltchev. This formidable Russian roll-call is far from complete, but it underscores the point graphically. In all things gymnastic, where Russia leads, others tend to follow, or to be more accur-

ate, tended to follow. Recently, the intensive training methods so skilfully developed by the Russians have ceased to be sufficient to secure their leadership of gymnastics because their rivals, having examined their techniques, have adapted and refined them to suit their own requirements. This has resulted in a much needed and most refreshing variety of skills and attitudes throughout the sport.

To the uninitiated, Eastern Europe is an homogenous entity — they are all communist, therefore they are all the same. Little could be further from the truth. True, eight out of every ten top gymnasts are from Eastern Europe, but within that bloc exist historical and cultural rivalries which are discernible in the sporting postures of these different states. There is a complex mosaic of nationalistic animosity between those states that are under the Soviet Union's influence, in many cases as a matter of constriction rather than conviction. The healthy independence of spirit of countries like Romania, Poland, or Hungary is most safely given expression in sporting arenas, and gymnastics competitions provide a fine opportunity for this. As we shall see later, these rivalries do sometimes spill over into public view and when that happens, a very sour sports spectacle is the result.

One of the reasons for the consistency of standards in this group of countries is that they all pursue the same ideological path, with the aid of almost identical educational systems. The pattern of lower and higher education is well established and varies little. Thus a continuity has been created which, while inflexible and therefore

Takuji Hayata of Japan showing why he won the rings gold medal at the Tokyo Olympic Games.

Left:
Boris Shakhlin on the rings at the 1966 World Championships in Dortmund.

slow to adapt to new needs, does ensure an enormous depth of experience and expertise in traditional areas of interest. All sporting activities come under this system, and because sport is given a high educational, social, and cultural priority, students of gymnastics are granted every possible facility. Indeed, in most formally structured educational programs, physical education is given a high priority; because of the discipline involved, performance can be carefully monitored, and faults corrected before they become ingrained. In a more liberal school system, unless there is a club coach helping outside the curriculum, some of these problematic faults may go unchecked, hampering the gymnast as he or she attempts to progress. In countries like Japan, West Germany, and the United States, an ordered,

though not so rigidly structured, educational system combines with an attitude that encourages the pursuit of individual achievement and a degree of self-gratification. The pursuit of individual reward is discouraged by the socialist states, but is considered essential to a competitive philosophy as practised eleswhere.

In the Soviet Union or East Germany a talented gymnast will be encouraged to persevere with the sport if the State considers that by so doing he or she is serving it in a useful way. However much that gymnast enjoys the sport, should he fall short of the standards that the State sets he will not be able to continue, and will be encouraged to seek an alternative interest that better suits his abilities and its requirements. From the State's point of view, to do otherwise would

It's all over, the medals have been won, thoughts revolve around victory and defeat; everyone being left to reflect on the events of the week.

be a waste of valuable resources which can be better utilized by someone else. It is unquestionably an élitist system despite the socialist bent of its ideology. States like Romania, which show more concern for the needs of the individual child, are similarly limited in the facilities available, but spend a higher proportion of the national budget on the development of recreational amenities, in an attempt to extend the benefits of their use as widely as possible.

We are at present witnessing the emergent Chinese developing a system that bears many similarities to the Romanian model. This is due in no small measure to the close links that have been created between the two peoples in social, cultural, scientific, and sporting spheres. Their educational systems bear many similarities, and the shared experiences of these two disparate countries have resulted in some great virtuosity and originality in gymnastics and its teaching. We can expect the mantle that for so long has been worn by the Russians to be resting on new shoulders by the middle

of the eighties, as China continues to develop its human resources in the field of gymnastics.

In the more enlightened and affluent of the Western countries, most recreational activity is driven by private industry, with the profit motive as its navigator. The less well-off usually find access to the best facilities that those countries offer restricted and beyond their financial reach. Progressive local authorities, educational and commercial institutions have started to help by assisting in the subsidy or creation of gymnastics centers as the sport has gained in popularity and prestige. Thus, while the State controls sports in the Communist bloc, private enterprise or enlightened public institutions dominate in the West. However, most Western countries enjoy some degree of government subsidy of sports by direct or indirect means, especially where complex facilities are needed to sustain a strong amateur arm.

Many areas of the world show little interest in or knowledge of gymnastics:

Right:
The East German competitor, Erika Zuchold, on the apparatus which has a circling movement named after her.

Some of the principal architects of the Prague crisis face the ordeal of a press conference, in order to justify the final decision of the vault judges.

46

Africa, South-west Asia, Oceania. In some cases these nations are intimately concerned with the basic problems of survival against a background of extremely scarce natural and financial resources. Gymnastics can hardly expect even a casual thought when food and shelter are not guaranteed on a daily basis, or where the economies are so small that they have little chance of affording sports a high priority.

As far as the African continent is concerned, gymnastics is not a widely supported sport. There has recently been an increase of interest and participation in South Africa, but that country's general political isolation, which in recent years has been carried through into sports and culture, has hindered its ability to develop the quality of its promising gymnasts. Lack of international competition at the highest representative level is a severe obstacle to any country trying to advance the bounds of its sporting ability. There is also an increasing interest in gymnastics in some of the North African countries, Egypt in particular.

With regard to the countries of Southwest Asia, there are some unusual reasons for a lack of progress in the development of the sport. Israel is certainly the most advanced of these States in the field of gymnastics and shows considerable expertise in its promotion. Many of the other countries in this area of the world are governed by restrictive Islamic law, and it is this fact that has curtailed the progress of the sport. There are some male gymnasts in Islamic countries who usually receive coaching from other lands with more experience of international competition. The aspect of Islamic law that has the most profound effect is that which governs the conduct and appearance of women. A display of gymnastics (as we know it) by women would be thought outrageous by orthodox religious leaders. A woman wearing a leotard, performing a simple exercise in public, would be considered shameless and immoral. There is most assuredly no equality of opportunity between the sexes built into the Islamic creed.

Australia and New Zealand are both countries with a recently increased gymnastics population and their standards are continually improving. Their greatest problem arises from their geographic isolation from all the major competitive countries. It is just too expensive to send or invite gymnasts to or from Europe or America. The

enormous distances between major population centers within both countries is an even more fundamental barrier to the smooth development of the sport. Just imagine the headaches that must exist in trying to organize a training weekend for a national squad consisting of team-members from Darwin, Melbourne, and Adelaide. Pockets of population separated by huge distances deter a continuity and regularity of training program so essential to the development of a national team as a world force.

Alongside the progress of gymnastics south of the North American border have come similar improvements in the standard of Canadian exponents. Much of this can be directly linked to the knock-on effect of hosting the Olympic Games in Montreal in 1976. The unprecedented genius of Nadia Comaneci's performance at these Games, and the excitement that she generated, added even more impetus to the already awakening desire to create a good, internationally competitive squad. Gymnastics is still increasing in popularity in Canada, and its team's performance at the Commonwealth Games in Edmonton gave a hint of the talent it has to offer the sport. As in many other fields, Canada draws incentive from a friendly yet deep-rooted desire to beat its better served neighbor to the south.

We are all waiting for a resurgence of the Scandinavian and Finnish prowess that dominated the men's events until the mid-fifties. It seems that we still have a while to wait, but, having fallen right back for twenty years, they are beginning to draw level with second-league forces like Great Britain, Italy, France and Spain. The West Germans are still the strongest competitors that Western Europe can muster but can never expect to compete as well as their Eastern counterparts so long as sports continue to receive a lower priority on the western side of the Wall.

It is worth remembering, however, that all is not well between the ideologically identical socialist states in Eastern Europe. The most dramatic expression of the discord that seethes beneath the surface of this most beautiful and expressive of sports came in the Prague European Championships in 1977.

After the excitement of Montreal, everyone was eagerly anticipating the Women's European event in which the leading gymnasts of the world, who at this time were

A characteristic pose from Nadia Comaneci's old floor routine.

Future champions at Sports School number 2 in Bucharest.

all Europeans, would be once again locked in a fiercely contested battle. The Olympic gold-medallists, Comaneci and Kim, were undoubtedly the greatest attraction and their battle for supremacy was the subject of much argument and speculation among pundits prior to the start of the competition. Many were adamant that Nadia could never repeat her phenomenal success, having achieved perfection in the eyes of the Montreal judges, she could only get worse, not better. As far as Nadia was concerned, such people were ill-informed fools, and she has never suffered fools gladly. Nelli, too, had much to prove; she had also been given a perfect score on two occasions at the Olympics and was a more experienced competitor than her great Romanian rival. Nadia's close friend and compatriot Teodora Ungureanu was another medal prospect and there were some other Russian gymnasts in very definite contention, such as Maria Filatova and the new discovery Elena Mukhina. The standing of the personal reputations that were at stake was

such as to guarantee world-wide interest in what in essence was a rather parochial event.

For all the ballyhoo that surrounded the Montreal scores, it is now generally recognized by experts that the judging was rather lax, and that overgenerous marking in the earlier stages of the event inevitably led to the awarding of the first-ever perfect scores. Prior to every competition, the judges meet in order to establish the standard to which they will mark and to try to agree their approach to the more subjective areas of the scoring system. The 'Code of Points', the handbook for judges, lists all the faults to be watched for and the penalties they incur. Even with the Code, however, there are many aspects of a performance left to a purely subjective interpretation and response from each of the judges. How one judge perceives 'amplitude' or 'the general impression' of an exercise may vary markedly from another's view. Indeed, this is inevitable in every sport that relies on subjective judging, though whether it is the

Left:
Svetlana Grozdova of the USSR in a dramatic floor exercise.

Right:
Vera Cerna of Czechoslovakia on her best apparatus.

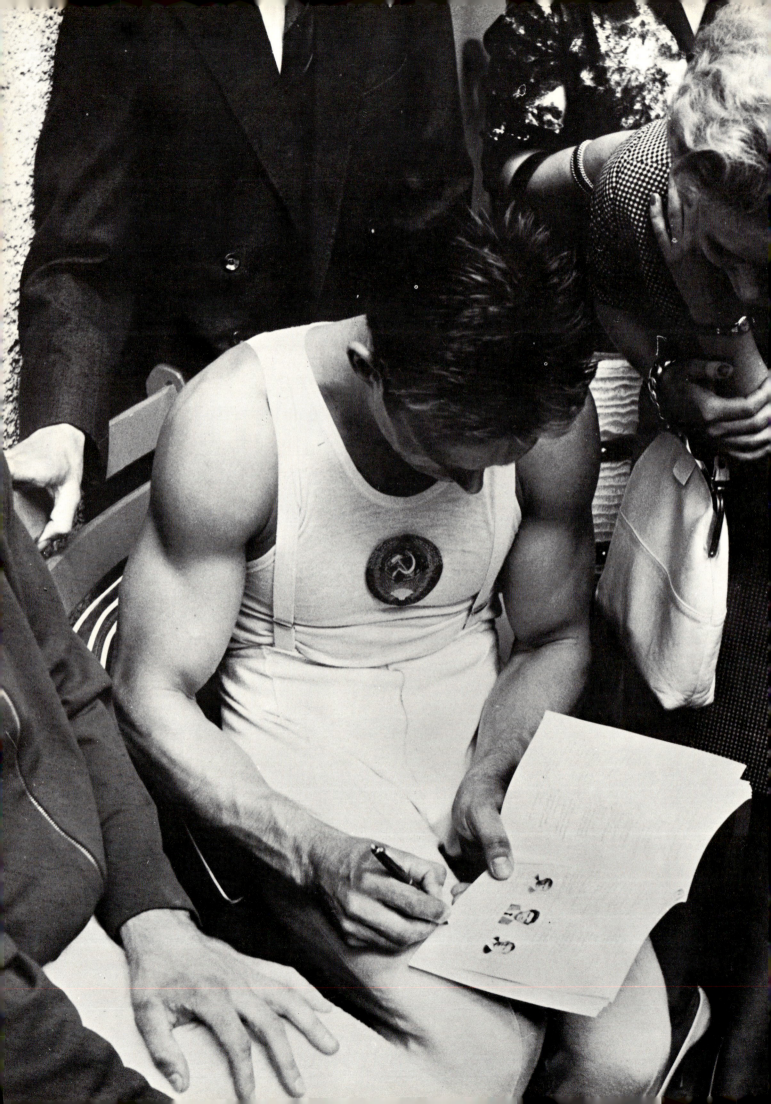

only reason for the baffling disparity in marks that sometimes occurs is a moot point.

The decision had been taken at Prague that in that competition, the judging would be more critical than at Montreal, and a common approach was sought. However, what no members of the public knew was that some months prior to this competition, some senior Soviet officials had indicated that they were not too pleased with the fact that the Romanian team, and Nadia in particular, were beginning to eclipse the carefully nurtured popularity of their women's team. In addition to being champions in their own right, their successful athletes are frequently used by the Soviet Government as ambassadors of 'good will' and prestige, and it was therefore a matter of priority to the Russians to ensure that the impact of their star gymnasts be fully maintained. In view of the fact that the challenge to their supremacy came from one of their Warsaw Pact neighbors, casual observers could have been forgiven for assuming that the Russians would not mind handing over the titles for a while to a nation with similar ideology. Nothing could have been further from the truth. Because that country was Romania, which has always been something of an anomaly and a renegade within the Soviet system. Romania is a fiercely independent member of the Warsaw Pact, boasting, as it does, complete sovereignty over its armed forces and its territory, the strongest and oldest church system, and considerable independence in the formulation of its foreign policy. None of these factors endear it to the Kremlin. And by the start of the European Championships in Prague the Romanian team had become a symbol of Romanian independence and deservedly so.

News began to filter through from East Germany at the beginning of 1977 that a confrontation was going to be engineered at the Prague Championships; at the same time, informed rumors started to circulate in Switzerland and West Germany that pressure was being applied on the more susceptible Eastern Bloc sports ministries to adopt 'a continuity of approach to the judging of performance of all friendly federations', the key word being 'friendly'. It must be realized that these machinations have nothing whatsoever to do with the individual gymnasts, few of whom are even aware that such scheming can occur behind the scenes.

Before the competition started, in the hotels and at small private gatherings, the 'judges' bargaining' got down to the customary nitty-gritty of exchanges of favors. While never officially admitted, such sessions *do* occur and, in theory at least, can help in further standardizing the various national interpretations of the 'Code of Points'. But, of course, they also provide the setting for the kind of 'if you score favorably towards our gymnasts, we will score favorably . . . ' trading that audiences speculate must be the explanation for scoring aberrations, yet at the same time cannot quite believe could happen. The plain fact is, that any sport that is decided by judges – whether gymnastics, ice-skating or high-diving – holds itself open to this kind of abuse. Gymnastics has just introduced a radically revised Code of Points designed to remove as much leeway as possible, and it will remain to be seen how well the new Code works.

The European vault finals, under the old Code, were to provide observers with proof of all the under-the-counter bargaining that had preceded them, and gave credence to the rumors mentioned earlier. Nelli Kim and Nadia Comaneci were the innocent pawns in the ever uglier situation that developed. The gymnastic controversy at the heart of the incident concerned the marks awarded by the judges for the better of the two vaults performed by the girls. Nelli executed a technically more complex vault, but failed to spot the landing without a step back and, suffering a minor break in form, landed slightly off center – nevertheless a very fine exercise. Nadia attempted a less complex vault, but her execution was superior to that of her rival. The judges were in disagreement and the head judge called for a conference in order to try and resolve the difference in the scores. A protest over the marks was lodged and heated discussions ensued amongst the judges; at that stage, Yuri Titov, the Soviet ex-gymnast who is the head of the FIG, became involved. The result was farcical and contemptible: Nadia, with the better vault, was downmarked into the silver medal position. The audience was far from happy, some of the judges were upset, and certain team officials were furious at a blatant subversion of sporting principles. Showing the sportsmanship that distinguishes athletes from the machinations of some behind-the-scenes interests, the two girls carried on with the competition as

The Soviet former World Champion, Yuri Titov, observing the ritual of the autograph for one of his many followers. He is currently the President of the International Gymnastics Federation (FIG).

55

Above:
The popular 1979
world champion,
Nelli Kim.

Left:
Nadia Comaneci
performing the
Comaneci somersault.

Far left:
Stoian Deltchev of
Bulgaria.

Right:
Kathy Johnson of the
USA dismounting from
the bars.

Left:
One of the greatest of all Soviet gymnasts, Larissa Latynina, working on the asymmetric bars at the 1966 World Championships. These old-fashioned sets of bars would not survive the pounding of contemporary exercises.

Typical of the camaraderie that pervades the sport, the three medalists in the beam finals at the World Championships share their success, under the kindly eye of President Lubke in Dortmund. From left to right the girls are Larissa Petrik (bronze), Vera Caslavska (silver), and Natasha Kuchinskaya (gold).

if nothing were untoward.

This sorry event, coming on top of other minor irritations during the championship, had been enough to convince the Romanians that they were not being treated fairly and, moreover, were unlikely to find that situation changing. In the event, it was hardly surprising that the immediate withdrawal of the team was ordered. Unannounced, the team left the competition hall, and because this was without the permission of the head judge, the team was disqualified and faced suspension from competition under the rules of the FIG. An inquiry was set up later in that year, the result of which was to overturn the disqualification and allow the Romanians to keep the medals that they had won. That incident, more than any other, gave impetus to the movement to amend the Code for judges, with a view to preventing a repetition of the conditions that led to a spectacle that did gymnastics such a disservice.

Probably the most famous, or infamous,

example of politics getting the better of sport occurred in 1963, when France hosted the Women's European Championships. The French authorities refused to allow the East German athletes to enter the country, and, in a mass demonstration of political support, all the Soviet-aligned states in Eastern Europe boycotted the event. Yugoslavia was the only Eastern representative to compete (doing rather well, as it happens).

As suggested earlier, one of the most exciting aspects of the current world scene in gymnastics is that the previously predictable areas of dominance such as the USSR, East Germany, Japan and Czechoslavakia can no longer expect to have things all their own way. The renaissance of Chinese involvement has breathed new life and new ideas into the sport. Not since Russia started participating fully has so significant a development occurred and the timing could hardly have been better. Many people who have enjoyed watching, or participating in, gymnastics over the past decade had noticed that much of the fun and exuberance of earlier times had disappeared from the sport at international level. Spontaneity had been suspended by a mechanical approach to training, competing, and thinking. The flair of the Americans, the innovation of the Chinese, and the unbelievable zest of the Cubans, all point to a rekindling of the spirit of enjoyment and the reawakening of self-expression, both of which are ready victims when a sport gains in media importance and loses its ethos.

The nations that have dominated gymnastics for so long are going to have to prepare themselves for the challenge of a new era of more open competition. This will unquestionably benefit the sport, which has stagnated a little during decades when the only uncertainty was which protegé would take over from a retiring champion.

It is in an atmosphere of healthy, open competition that sports, as many other spheres of life, thrive. With all the external threats to the established order, and the fact that so much prestige is at stake, the immediate future in gymnastics promises to be as dynamic as the period that followed Olga at Munich. It only needs one or two individuals with the courage to try new ideas and the whole scene could undergo a revolution; gymnastics is a sport that lends itself to producing virtuosi with the flair to extend the frontiers of both human achievement and the sport itself.

60

5 A Gymnastics Hall of Fame

Having surveyed the balance of world strength in gymnastics in general terms, we will put some of the major powers under a more penetrating microscope in a later chapter. Next, we will focus on some of the outstanding exponents of the sport, past and present, in terms of the lasting achievements and influence with which they have graced gymnastics, helped shape and improve it at top competition level, extended its horizons and introduced it to new legions of enthusiasts through the dynamic artistry of their performances.

The most basic way to identify the sport's innovators is to thumb through a coaching or judging manual, picking out all the elements and movements with personal names as part of their descriptions. If one were to overhear a coach talking about the correct way to execute a Tsukahara, the assumption that he is training a gangland hit-man for a contract in Japan may be hasty. He is just as likely to be referring to the vault named after its Japanese originator.

There are others in the hall-of-fame who have never had a movement named after them but are remembered with equal respect and affection. These are the gymnasts that have competed with such consistent excellence over several years, and on most of the pieces of apparatus, that their sheer brilliance outshone any lack of inventiveness. In gymnastics, as in other sports, there are also several examples of great characters whose virtuosity and vibrant personality so endeared them to the public that deficiencies in performance were hardly noticed and are quickly forgiven by memory.

For the men, let us start with the name of Stalder. His name is associated with a move on the high-bar, and on the asymmetric-bars by many of the leading women; it involves circling from a handstand, through a straddle support, back to a handstand. The originator of this element was a Swiss gymnast called Josef Stalder who competed internationally in early post-war years. He was awarded an Olympic gold medal in 1948 for his high-bar exercise, and was a gold medallist at the 1950 World Championships. He, and the Swiss team, also took several medals at the 1952 Olympic Games.

Changing apparatus for the moment, we move to the creator of the Azarian crucifix or Azarian iron-cross, as it is usually termed these days. Unlike a conventional crucifix, in Azarian's the head, trunk and legs are turned side-on to the rings, consequently requiring greater strength. Its originator was Albert Azarian, a leading Soviet gymnast of the mid-fifties to the beginning of the sixties. As it happens, his son Edward is a current member of the Soviet national squad and is including his father's element in his rings exercise.

The Diamidov turn is a great feature of modern parallel bars exercises. It involves executing a 360 degree turn in the handstand position, while keeping one hand firmly on the bars. The man first responsible for the movement, the Soviet gymnast Sergei Diamidov, competed in the mid to late sixties.

Although the legendary Yugoslavian, Miroslav Cerar, and that dynamic American Kurt Thomas have both made dramatic impacts on the pommelled horse exercise, the

*Nadia demonstrating
her version of a free
walkover in training,
April 1978.*

*Right:
Sergei Diamidov of
the Soviet Union
demonstrating the turn
on parallel bars that is
named after him.*

man whose name is synonymous with the pommelled horse is the Hungarian gymnast, Zoltan Magyar. He is the originator of the Magyar walk, which is a reference to his travel along all three sections of the horse. His complete technical mastery of this apparatus has been unmatched in recent years, even by the exuberant Thomas (who has given the exercise the flairs which now bear his name).

When one considers the vault, two modern movements come immediately to mind. The first is the Yamashita vault, named after the top Japanese gymnast, Haruhiro Yamashita, who revealed it at the World Championships in 1962. It is most unlikely that one will see a basic Yamashita performed at any major competition nowadays because, even if perfectly executed, it will not merit a maximum score. Such is the relentless progress in gymnastics that the Yamashita is already thought to lack sufficient technical difficulty.

The second name associated with the vault is that of Tsukahara. This complex vault involves a backward somersault off the horse in the second flight phase which may be tucked, piked, straight, or twisting. It was first demonstrated by the Japanese competitor, Mitsuo Tsukahara.

The women have also been responsible for their share of innovation. Three East German girls have lent their names to movements in the asymmetric bars exercises, these being Karen Janz for the Janz roll, Brigit Radochla for her somersault and Erika Zuchold for the Zuchold circle. Of all of these movements, the one most widely recognized by audiences is the Radochla somersault, though nowadays more often in a variant version. Originally, the Radochla, which is a front somersault with the legs in side-straddle, was performed from the low bar to grasp the high bar. However, a new and more daring variety has been developed by the Romanian gymnast, Nadia Comaneci, which is, not surprisingly, becoming known as the Comaneci somersault. This is performed exclusively on the high-bar, with the re-grasp completely unsighted — a very good reason for it being one of the most frightening moves in any gymnastic repertoire.

One of the most fallible of the world's leading gymnasts was that effervescent Soviet heroine of 1972, Olga Korbut. The audiences were completely spellbound by her extrovert personality, diminutive size,

The incomparable Zoltan Magyar of Hungary on his favorite piece of apparatus.

her daring and virtuosity. Although she could manipulate an audience at will, the judges were not so easily moved. Olga was always a greater personality than a technically sound competitor, her temperament being unsuited to the demands of total concentration that is an essential component in the make-up of today's top gymnasts. Apart from her friendly disposition, she is remembered for two particular movements on two separate pieces of apparatus. Firstly, on the asymmetric bars, her famous aerial leap on the high-bar. To be more precise, this was a flic-flac executed from a momentary squat stand on the high-bar, to regrasp and hang from that same bar. The second movement that Olga immortalized, largely because it appeared so risky, was her standing backward somersault on the beam, which drew gasps of amazement from the auditoria in her day. Alas (in some ways), this once-defiant movement has already become commonplace among even junior gymnasts. Perhaps we should include a third movement

of Olga's which also occurred on the balance beam, for, with the two other movements, it serves to illustrate an interesting technical point. So marked was the suppleness of her spine, and particularly the lower back, that with her chest and chin resting on the top of the beam, she could gradually bring her legs over her head until they were virtually parallel with it, her backside resting on the crown of her head. In this movement, as always, she exhibited perfect extension, tension and suppleness. However, each stage produced a break in the rhythm of her program, sometimes to an extent that warranted a deduction from her score according to the Code of Points. Olga tended to pause to set herself up for each stage of the movement, a fault she has unfortunately left as a legacy to many contemporary exponents of the somersault on the beam who covet Olga's tremendous popularity and try to emulate her.

Indeed, Olga's enduring influence on the style of women's gymnastics is viewed with criticism in some quarters of the sport. Her gamine appearance and precocious personality played a major part in her popular appeal, and the warmth of the public reaction to her, tempted many coaches in the mid- and late seventies to model some of their talented girls on Olga. This has been responsible for a gradual shift from the classical, balletic form of gymnastics typified by the Latyninas, Caslavskas and Turischevas to the more elfin performances of the Korbuts, Filatovas and Comanecis, a change that many purists decry. But, for the moment, Korbut and her followers have certainly captured the imagination of gymnastics fans, which is evidenced by the fact that in post-Olga years Comaneci and Nelli Kim have succeeded in attracting the popularity that has somehow eluded the great Turischeva.

Certainly, in 1972, Olga Korbut gave the sport a new vitality, and her own charismatic efforts have been more responsible than anthing else for attracting a wider following. Mercifully, having recently become a mother, she has had to abandon ill-conceived plans for a comeback. Hers is a story tinged with some sadness. Propelled suddenly, and unexpectedly, into the role of the world's most popular sportswoman and a leading ambassadress for the Soviet Union, she was unable to cope, her mental and physical health taking a terrible battering. Returning to London after presenting her

The elfin Olga, to whom gymnastics owes so much; for her cheeky charm was largely responsible for the renaissance of the sport.

*Haruhiro Yamashita,
who has a vault named
after him as its first
exponent, is seen here
demonstrating his
prowess on the parallel
bars.*

with an award from the British viewing public, a leading English sports journalist told a harrowing tale about his meeting with Olga. It took place in a sanatorium, the little gymnast being a haggard shell of her normal, outgoing self. She broke down the moment she was asked to say a few words on accepting the trophy, but her tears were of anguish rather than joy. She exhibited all the signs of mental and physical exhaustion. Since that time she has had to retire several times to regain her health and emotional stability in a sanatorium, and one can only reflect that the pressures on such young people (remember, Olga was only 14 at Munich) of training, preparing new routines and participating in the round of established competitions are great enough without adding the burden of being a show-piece for a vain, publicity-conscious government.

One name that is synonymous with all that is good in gymnastics is that of the Czechoslovakian competitor of the 1960s, Vera Caslavska. The gymnastics fraternity has never had cause to speak ill of her, either as a person or as a gymnast. According to Maria Simionescu, that most respected of international judges and senior official of the FIG, Vera was arguably the finest all round gymnast of her day, surpassing her former arch-rival, the Russian, Laryssa Latynina, in overall presentation. The most recent major exponent of Caslavska's classical style was that most elegant of Korbut's teammates, Ludmilla Turischeva. She followed in Vera's style of balletic gymnastics and impeccable sportsmanship.

Vera was the protegé of the leading Czech woman's gymnast, Eva Bosakova. Vera was born in 1942 and retired from the sport in 1968 at the height of her success. Such are

69

j&f HOLLAND

As you can see, there was no lack of amplitude in Karin Janz's leap on the beam at the 1967 European Championships. She was one of the best women produced by the East Germans.

the physical and emotional demands of the sport today that few girls would expect to be competing at top level at Vera's retirement age of 26. Her first real success was in Krakow at the European Championships of 1959 at which she won a first gold medal, for her beam exercise, at the age of 17. However, one of the more remarkable facts about her career is that it did not really get underway until she was 22 years of age, at the 1964 Tokyo Olympics. There she earned three gold medals and one silver to become the overall champion. She also became overall champion in the next two European Championships, the 1966 World Championship, and the 1968 Mexico Olympic Games, after which she announced her retirement. After the gymnastics event was over, she married one of her compatriots in the athletics team, Josef Odlozel, in the Mexico City Cathedral. Her personal victory in the Olympics of 1968 was one of the few moments of happiness for the Czech people in that tragic and traumatic year. The Soviet Union and its Warsaw Pact allies, with the exception of Romania, invaded her country and instituted a savage repression against the more liberal elements of Czech society.

Vera Caslavska was an innovator, and introduced several new moves on bars and beam. However, the general public remember her for her charm, poise, elegance, and great agility. She was a master of all the pieces of apparatus in her time, and was technically a superb gymnast.

We now come to the most remarkable talent in the history of gymnastics, the Romanian girl – Nadia Comaneci. Hardbitten, seen-it-all-before sports commentators and journalists have called her the finest gymnast every known. It is not difficult to make out a strong case for such an accolade. Nadia was born in November 196_ in Onesti, a small provincial town in Romania. She first came to the attention of the world at the Champions All competition, held annually in London, in April 1975. She was not yet thirteen and a half, but she swept all before her and won the competition as a complete unknown. What better way to make one's debut on the international scene? Shortly afterwards the European Championships were held in Skien, Norway, and Nadia and her teammates were pitted against the pre-competition joint favorites, the Russians and the East Germans. With Turischeva and Kim leading the Russian assault on the medals, and Zinke

and Schmeisser following suit for the East Germans, who else could expect a look-in for the overall and individual medals? Suffice to say that Nadia won three golds and a silver in the apparatus finals, and became European Overall Champion. This was a case of unmitigated impudence in someone not yet fourteen years old, and how the audiences loved it!

At Montreal in the 1976 Olympic Games, Nadia made Olympic and gymnastics history. At the tender age of fourteen and a half, she became the youngest ever Olympic champion, picking up the beam and bars gold medals as well as the Individual Overall title. She created further history by becoming the first gymnast to be awarded a perfect score of 10 points, repeating this amazing feat on no less than seven occasions during the competition. The Russian gymnast, Nelli Kim, no doubt spurred on by the example set by Nadia, picked up two perfect marks herself. Since Montreal, Nadia

One of the best all-round competitors that the Russians have produced, Ludmilla Turischeva, whose charming personality endeared her to the public wherever she went. She married Valery Borzov, the sprinter, and has since become a mother as well as a top coach.

has continued to receive perfect scores at many other major international matches.

During the onset of puberty, she gained much height and weight and her performance suffered accordingly. It was at this time that much of the world's press wrote her off as a gymnast. However, it was just at this stage of her life that she became arguably the greatest athlete in the world, for despite a dramatic morphological change in her body, she was able to fight back to competitive form. Few people are aware of the immensity of this achievement. For Nadia to regain her former supremacy, indeed to surpass it in certain areas, can be likened to a 9.9 second 100 meter sprinter being able to match his best time dressed in full army combat gear.

Nadia took her third successive European title, for despite the wrangling in Prague she won the 1977 Championship, in Copenhagen in 1979 and in so doing made history yet again, for no one had previously managed a hat-trick. With its sights firmly set on the Moscow Olympics the Romanian team traveled to Texas at the end of 1979 for the World Championships which would act as a qualifying event for Moscow. Sadly, the eagerly anticipated confrontation between Nadia and her Russian rivals, Mukhina, Shaposhnikova, and Kim, never materialized because a wrist infection hospitalized her. However, her teammates provided the

Above:
Nadia, the young Romanian girl destined to stand the world of women's gymnastics on its head. Here, she is seen for the first time in the West, at the Daily Mirror Champions All competition in London, 1975, which she won.

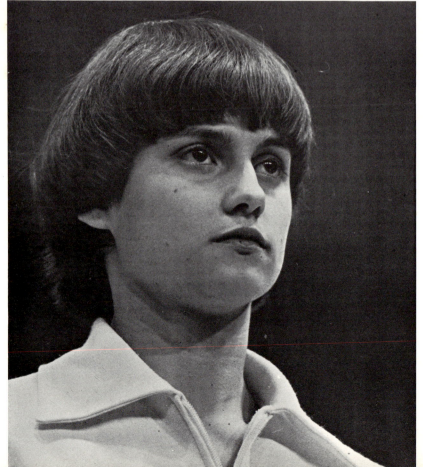

Right:
The brooding eyes of a troubled champion — Nadia was out of sorts with herself around the time of the Strasbourg World Championships.

Right:
The reborn Nadia, honed to near perfection. Enormous self-discipline is required of a girl in order to attain and keep this sort of shape after puberty.

sensation of the match by winning the team gold medal from the Soviet squad.

Despite rumors of retirement, in January 1980 Nadia recommenced her full training schedule in preparation for Moscow. No one can doubt her dedication to the sport. Nadia began in the mold of Olga Korbut, by virtue at least of her size and appearance, though the technical content and execution of her programs was always higher than those of her Soviet counterpart. Where Olga was demonstrative, Nadia has been impassive, and relatively unaffected by her success. With her more mature physique, she has moved from the gamine to the classical style, and her floor exercises in particular have shown a marked improvement as a result. Even more than Caslavska, Nadia will be remembered as an innovator, especially on the asymmetric bars, as well as an all-round master of the sport. Technically and mechanically she is difficult to fault, but perhaps her greatest weakness, especially now that character and personality are so much appreciated by audiences, is that at times she lacks expressiveness. The reason for her technical brilliance lies not so much in her innate gymnastic ability, but rather in her intensive training program and staggering work-rate.

As a little parlor game, it is interesting (though probably futile) to consider who was the greater gymnast — Caslavska or Comaneci. Any serious attempt to come to grips with that thorny question must relate their performance with the general standard of the sport at the highest levels at the time; they were both technically superior to their respective contemporaries. Their styles are vastly different and reflect the fashions as well as the state of the art of the time. Vera was the more feminine and expressive of the two, but then she was a mature woman, with a most elegant frame. Nadia is not yet out of her teens. In the author's view, Nadia Comaneci is slightly the more accomplished of the two; superior technique, a greater element of risk along with more complex exercises and the fact that these combined qualities have raised the level of women's gymnastics measurably, give the Romanian the edge.

Of course, all great gymnasts owe a large measure of their success to their coaches. The coach plays a big part in inspiring and constructing new routines and in giving his or her charge the confidence to attempt them.

6 The Coach

Frequently, at least for the duration of his or her career, the relationship between a top gymnast and his or her coach dominates normal family relationships. The coach becomes a surrogate parent to his pupils, the confidant to whom the gymnast turns for inspiration and confidence. In Iron Curtain systems, where gymnasts are removed from the family environment, to live and work in a closed sports educational community, this dependant relationship develops easily. Where the gymnast is tied closely to the family, there can often arise a period of friction between trainer and parents, which is bound to have a detrimental effect on the performance of the fledgling athlete. There have been many instances of parental coaches, but family teams of athlete and coach have not often proved outstandingly successful.

The root problem facing a parental coach is finding a way of separating family life from coaching duties. If a tense atmosphere develops between trainer and gymnast in the gymnasium, it is unlikely that the matter will be allowed to rest when they leave the training session, and is bound to cause some disruption of the domestic scene. The parent and child who can put an argument behind them at the dinner-table and avoid business begetting a bitter family row are enlightened indeed. Furthermore, a parent-coach and child-athlete teaming is often a sign of a thrusting, unfulfilled parent seeking to satisfy personal ambitions by proxy. It is neither uncommon nor unnatural for a parent to try to realize the unfulfilled goals of life through his or her children. All parents who coach their own children must be certain that self-interest is not blinding them to the best interests of their offspring.

It is rare to find any top gymnast who has been coached for a significant part of his competitive life by a parent, even when that parent is a national coach. At an early stage in a gymnastics career, a parent with some knowledge or experience of the sport may well set a budding gymnast on a training schedule. But in order to encourage the development of independence and a wider gymnastics experience, any child with the ability and inclination to work towards competitive achievement should swiftly separate training obligations from his social and domestic life. There are strong psychological justifications for this, both in terms of the well-being of relationships within the family, and to allow the child to pass through the normal psycho-sexual stages in a natural manner, avoiding any problems in its character formation. As every parent knows, at stages in its development a child will respond to one parent more than the other, seek peer groups outside the family and sometimes even reject the family and the ties it represents. These are difficult times for all concerned, but they are a natural part of the process of growing up and carving out one's own identity. The wisest parents with a gymnastics (or indeed any sports) background recognize the changes of the seemingly obvious step of coaching their own children, and avoid them. Albert Azarian, the brilliant Soviet gymnast, now a national coach, has kept well away from coaching his son Edward, himself currently a leading member of the Soviet Olympic squad.

Nadia and former coach, Gheorghe Condovice, practising her double-back on floor. Remembering that this was in April 1978, when she was a little heavy, it is difficult to believe that her center of gravity is over eight feet from the ground and that the jump is unaided.

Men dominate top level coaching in both men's and women's gymnastics. This is to some extent the legacy of gymnastics history, the sport in its infancy having been an exclusively male preserve in competition. With the instrusion of women into the sport, the pattern altered little. The involvement of women in coaching tended to be restricted to the early stage of a gymnast's development when the emphasis is on body preparation, with the men continuing to govern the delicate process of bringing top prospects to competition standard. There are now many more women coaches at all levels of the sport, though, not surprisingly, it is unusual to find a woman coaching men. They frequently train boys at early club level, offering just the right skills to aid the development of body-tension, suppleness, and co-ordination of movement. However, as a boy hopeful approaches and moves through his teens, the psychological and

physical demands of men's gymnastics ensure that a male coach will be of greatest benefit to his progress. Within the confines of the gymnasium, the attitude of the youth to his coach must reflect complete trust, respect, and occasionally a little fear. The coach must be able to rely upon the mental, physical, and emotional energies of his student being channeled one hundred percent into training and the arduous task of preparing for the competition hall. The danger of the parent's role being usurped to some degree by the coach is ever-present, one of the inevitable factors in a sports career. As long as the youth remains within the family unit, the situation tends to resolve itself as part of the natural process of growing up.

One powerful argument in favor of male coaches is power itself, the greater strength of men than women. A self-evident observation certainly, but one that has a direct

Bela Karoly leaving no doubt in Teodora's mind as to what he expects from her performance.

bearing on the trust that a gymnast has in his or her coach. A gymnast about to attempt an untried complex or dangerous movement requiring the support of a coach is liable to feel more confident of avoiding injury if there is a man waiting to catch him.

It is a fact that nearly all the greatest names in women's gymnastics have been trained by men for the major part of their competitive lives. The finest women coaches, who tend to be ex-gymnasts of the caliber of the Russian trainers, Latynina or Turischeva, are still very much in the minority amidst the championship medal prospects for the future. Girl and women athletes still respond better, in the main, to male teachers.

In the sphere of outstanding coaches one turns naturally to two names, the Soviet, Rastorotsky, and the Romanian, Karoly. Both men have evoked critical comment about their Svengali-like influence over the young girls in their charge. Such anxiety is rooted more in lack of understanding, often fuelled by professional jealousy, than hard fact, though the existence of a strong bond between trainer and pupil is undeniable.

One major advantage that these men enjoy over their western counterparts is that they teach gymnastics in a closed community and can exercise considerable control over the environment to which their protégées are subjected. The immense respect and power that they command within their

Nik Stuart, the best gymnast ever to represent Great Britain up amongst the rafters. On retirement from competition, he turned to coaching and is one of the most respected and best loved personalities in the world of sport.

Neither the competitor or his coach look too pleased with his exercise.

77

The monologue is mightier than the dialogue. A senior coach, impressing a point upon his listeners.

Left:
Bill McLoughlin and Avril Lennox in a training session before the 1977 Prague Championships.

respective federations affords them the right to select those who will enter the élite squads and schools that are their responsibility. They both know that they will only be offered the finest, physically suitable material to work with, so that they are free to screen the hopefuls for what they consider personality weaknesses. The girls that they tend to choose are those with whom they can expect to establish a good rapport. Because of the esteem in which they are held, these coaches can expect to have the best available facilities placed at their disposal as well as a first-rate back-up staff of choreographers, coaches, doctors, dieticians, physiotherapists, musical arrangers, and the like.

Rastorotsky and Karoly both have an unsurpassed intuitive understanding of the mechanics of gymnastics, and a natural em-

pathy for the sport itself. Their depth of knowledge of, and innovatory genius for, gymnastics sets them apart from their contemporaries. With their powerful personalities, they are able to motivate and energize their charges. To say that they rule by force of personality would be an over-simplification, but one not without a kernel of truth. They do become surrogate parents to the girls living within the sports complexes under their control, a circumstance which serves to strengthen the bond between coach and gymnast and helps to develop a deeper form of mutual trust and respect. Bela Karoly has a valuable lieutenant in his wife, Marta, a superb coach and judge in her own right, and Marta's involvement helps to underline the familial sort of relationship that pervades Karoly's squad.

Given the physical nature of the sport, it

is not surprising that sexual undertones are implied by some in the close contact that exists between the girls and young women and their male coaches, who tend to be considerably older than the trainees. Gymnastics is a sensual rather than overtly sexual sport, expressive as it is of the beauty of the human body, and many choreographers, aware of this, use its sensuality to stunning effect in the floor exercise. However, while at certain stages in a girl's emotional and physical development some of her motivation will come from a scarcely understood sexual response to her male coach, this seldom, if ever, leads to anything improper.

The role of a coach is a parental not a sexual one, and there has never been any (publicized) incident of a coach dishonoring his position of trust.

The fund of coaching talent is constantly being replenished by retired competitive gymnasts, so that one generation's expertise and technical advance is reinvested into the sport to be built upon by succeeding teams of trainee gymnasts and coaches with personal experience of the competition hall. In turn, many coaches become judges, helping to ensure that, in technical awareness and overall standard, these key officials do not lag far behind advances in the sport. After

Nik Stuart keeping a watchful eye on Tommy Wilson competing at Varna. As long as he does not block the view of the judges and gives no assistance to his charge during the exercise, the coach may remain on the podium. Safety is a major consideration in allowing his presence there.

Christina Itu sitting in the pit after landing there at the end of a tumbling sequence, while her coach, Gheorghe Gorgoi, proffers some advice. These pits are filled with vast quantities of foam rubber and are a great help when a gymnast needs to practice some new and risky dismounts.

the rather unpleasant disagreements among judges at some recent major internationals, one could be forgiven for thinking that extraneous factors are affecting judges' assessments of competitors' performances. Sadly, this seems to be increasingly the case. Earlier we looked at the incident that occurred in Prague during the 1977 European Championships. Part of the problem was that the 'Code of Points', which is the judging manual of the FIG, held itself open to deliberate misinterpretation because it was too vague and left far too much subjectivity in the scoring system. This has since been revised and tightened up; in future there will be open scoring akin to that in iceskating, so that each judge's marking is subject to public scrutiny.

Nothing in the Code of Points can rule out the nefarious practise of 'judges bargaining'. Prior to an event a group of officials can get together to pre-agree to steer scoring in some specific direction. The Soviet Union, for example, if it sees what it considers to be an unacceptable set of circumstances, can expect to use its considerable influence to achieve an environmental move conducive to its success. The way the judging panels were selected meant that there

was a very good chance that at least a few members could be relied on to assist the Russians ends. 'Bargaining' happens in many sports between competing countries, clubs, or almost any organizations. Despite all, the general standard of judging is improving, but because it remains a subjective matter, differences of interpretation and attitude will always be reflected in some erratic scoring. The artistic and sporting values of one country or one judge may bear little similarity to those of another, and thus an exercise which some consider to have been executed beautifully may seem unimpressive to others.

By now we have formed a picture of the complex interlocking society that is gymnastics, the many factors that have to come together before a talented youngster metamorphises into a title-winning gymnast. The sport makes great demands on the individual, whether as competitor, coach, judge, or administrator. One talented individual needs the support and encouragement of many people, bodies and organizations, and in many ways the success or otherwise of its athletes mirrors very accurately the enthusiasm with which governments enter the international sports arena.

7 Judging Gymnastics

In an earlier chapter, mention was made of the 'Code of Points' which is the book that contains the details about the scoring system for all competitive gymnastics. It is the judges' bible, and what it decrees is law, but in the past there was much wrangling about the correct interpretation of the rules laid down in it. In 1979, a new version was published which was expressly designed with two things in mind. Firstly, the old book had to be updated in order to cover many of the recent technical innovations within the new exercises being performed at all levels in the sport. Secondly, an attempt had to be made to try to remove some of the gray areas surrounding the most subjective parts of the previous Code which had given rise to many of the most bitter disagreements between judges.

In Artistic Gymnastics, there are two such Codes; one each for the men and the women. Both of these have recently been updated, although the changes to the men's Code are minor by comparison to those within the new women's version.

A closer look at the scoring systems that operate in gymnastics competitions may give us a better understanding of the reasons behind what the spectators often feel to be inexplicable judging. One of the first facts to be grasped is that the major championships are divided into three specific competitions. Competition 1 is the team competition. Both the women's and the men's teams are comprised of six competing gymnasts, however only the top five scores count towards the team total on each piece of apparatus. The maximum possible men's score is six hundred points, this figure representing the five qualifying competitors working on six pieces of apparatus twice (firstly for the Compulsory and then for the Voluntary Exercises); remembering that the maximum individual score attainable is ten points. The same method of calculation is used for the women, but their maximum is limited to four hundred points, as they only compete over four items of apparatus.

It is only in Competition 1 that compulsory exercises have to be done. These contain certain prescribed elements, which do not necessarily have to be executed in the same order, and which are determined by the FIG in four year cycles.

Competition 2 is designed to find the Individual Overall Champion. This means the competitor who has amassed the highest total score from all the different pieces of apparatus. The result for the women's competition at the 1972 Munich Olympics serves as an interesting example of the way this can work. Ludmilla Turischeva won the Individual Overall title but what made this unusual was the fact that she failed to win any of the apparatus gold medals. Her compatriot, Olga Korbut won two gold medals and a silver, and Karen Janz, an East German, won two gold and a bronze. Turischeva could only manage a silver and a bronze and yet she took the overall title. The reason for this lies in the way that the individual point totals from Competition 1 are combined with those achieved in Competition 2 in order to determine the final result.

The maximum number of points obtainable directly from Competition 2 is sixty for the men (ten for each of the six disci-

Lutz Hoffman of East Germany about to regrasp the high bar.

Three of the most senior officials of the FIG, Yuri Titov (USSR), Ellen Berger (DDR), and Maria Simionescu (Romania), in heated discussion after the dubious scoring of Kim and Comaneci's vaulting at the Prague '77 European Championships.

A video replay is brought to the aid of the adjudicators, yet against expectations, the decision goes against the better executed vault. This apparent injustice forced the withdrawal of the Romanian team in protest.

plines), and forty for the women (ten for each of their four disciplines). The points scored here are added to half of the individual total from Competition 1, thereby making a possible score of 120 points and 80 points for men and women respectively.

Competition 3 determines the winner for each of the pieces of apparatus, and is often referred to as the apparatus finals. Thus, there are six gold medals at stake for the men and four for the women. Whereas in Competition 2, three gymnasts per nation are permitted out of a total of 36 eligible, in Competition 3 the maximum allowed is two per country, along with the eight best-placed competitors from Competition 1. The next two in the rankings are to make themselves available as reserves.

Each piece of apparatus carries a possible score of ten points, to which is added half of the appropriate score from Competition 1, allowing a total achievable number of twenty points.

Let us now turn our attention to the actual scoring system, as laid down in the Code of Points, starting with a look at the men's system.

Natasha Kuchinskaya at the 1966 World Championships. Her sporting life was tragically cut short by illness, and her enormous potential never fully realized.

There is a uniform allocation of points for five of the six disciplines, the exception being the vault, by virtue of its brevity and the rudiments that go into it. Looking at the scoring break-down for the other pieces of apparatus will make this more apparent. It should be remembered that the men have to perform both compulsory and voluntary exercises. The compulsory exercises, as mentioned earlier, are predetermined by the FIG and consist of combinations of A and B difficulties as decided by their technical committee. Difficulties, or Value Parts, are divided into three categories — A, B and C. The A parts represent the simplest elements and combinations, B parts have a medium difficulty rating, and C parts are of a high or superior difficulty. Each A part has a potential value of 0.20 points, B part — 0.40, and C part can be worth 0.60 points; these being the maximum values, assuming perfect execution.

With the exception of the vault, which is marked directly from 10 points, the five disciplines are scored from this format in the voluntary excercises:

Difficulty	3.4
Execution	4.4
Combination	1.6
Risk, Originality and Virtuosity	0.6
Total	10.00

It must be remembered that in the first part of Competition 1, all the exercises are the compulsory ones set by the FIG and these are marked differently. Marks are awarded according to two factors, the first being the exactness of the performance in accordance with the pre-set routine, and the second is in respect of the technical proficiency and style exhibited in the course of the exercise. 9.8 points are allocated for this, and the balance 0.20 can be earned by a demonstration of virtuosity by the gymnast. Virtuosity, according to the FIG, is the complete mastery or domination of the technique of artistic gymnastics.

In the second part of Competition 1, and Competitions 2 and 3, all the exercises are voluntary, and it is in these events that the judging becomes complex and subject to variations of interpretation. Referring to the list showing the break-down of the scoring in these competitions, the first item is that of Difficulty. There are specific requirements for the number and type of Difficulties for each of the Competitions.

Competition	1B	2	3
Difficulties required	4A	3A	2A
	5B	4B	3B
	1C	2C	3C
Points value	3.4	3.4	3.4

The next item for consideration is that of Execution, with a maximum value of 4.4, which concerns the technical and stylistic content and performance of the exercise. Here the judges are looking for good extension, amplitude, posture, and complete command of all of the elements of the routine.

The third item is that of Combination. This has a maximum rating of 1.6 points, and refers to the way that the individual elements of the routines are linked into a complete exercise. It is important that the transition from a lesser Difficulty to a higher (superior) one is smooth, and in keeping with the rhythm of the exercise as a whole.

The final matter to be judged is that of ROV, these initials standing for Risk, Originality, and Virtuosity. The quality of Virtuosity has already been covered, so let us examine the element of Risk. Effectively, it is the inclusion of an element or combination for the purpose of gaining bonus points, which involves danger to the gymnast or to the security of his exercise. This bonus allocation for Risk is not designed to encourage recklessness, but rather a degree of daring in terms of performance, and a gamble in terms of the routine. This leaves us with Originality to define. It is self-evident for, as far as the work on a piece of apparatus is concerned, it would be considered as a form, element, or connection which transcends the known and creates a precedent. Each of the different qualities of ROV carries a possible score of 0.20 points.

An examination of the scoring system for women's gymnastics should bear in mind that the new Code for women has received

a major facelift and is much revised. The changes have been so profound that many judges have shown great difficulty in assimilating it, a fact that has been attested to by virtue of an inordinate number of judges' conferences at recent competitions.

As with the men, the women have to contest both compulsory and voluntary exercises which fall into exactly the same Competitions as the men's. The women, of course, have only to compete on four pieces of apparatus. Once again, excepting the vault, the exercises are scored according to a standard formula, which is now very different from the old Code. The formula is detailed below:

Difficulty	3.0
Bonus Points	0.5
Combination	2.5
Execution and Virtuosity	4.0
Total	10.00

This scoring system applies only to the voluntary work, the compulsory exercises being marked along the lines detailed for the men. The Difficulty allocation is made up of those A, B and C elements listed earlier. The requirements for each competition are outlined below:

Competition	1B	2	3
Difficulties required	6A	4A	2A
	3B	4B	2B
	1C	1C	3C
Points value	3.0	3.0	3.0

Each A part is worth 0.2, B part is valued at 0.4, and C part carries a maximum possible 0.6 points.

The next category in the formula is the Bonus Points section. This is sub-divided three ways. Firstly, there is an allowance of 0.2 points for the Originality factor, as outlined in the men's scoring section. Next, there is a further 0.2 to be gained by the introduction of Risk into the exercise. Risk is accorded a value part of 'C' in the table of Difficulties. Lastly, there is a final 0.1 points to be awarded for the additional inclusion of a C part, with or without Risk, though it should be emphasized that it does not pay to include more than one additional element purely with the hope of boosting the number of Bonus Points, for the 0.1 is awarded only once, regardless of further inclusions. Interestingly, alongside Originality, there is also Rare Value which, as with

Originality, if combined with a C element, can earn Bonus Points, although this is seldom seen.

Combination is the next factor, with an allocation of 2.5. This figure is broken down into sub-sections which pertain to the distribution of elements through the exercise, its composition, and the rhythm, space, direction and tempo of the whole routine.

The last elements to be considered are Execution and Virtuosity. The Execution is judged according to the perfection of technique, posture, and amplitude and can win 3.8 for the competitor. Thus, 0.2 is available for the display of Virtuosity.

Having now obtained a picture of the way that the scoring is determined, there is little point in going into how each of the hundreds of different elements in all the various apparatus exercises is examined, analysed and marked, for that in itself would fill several volumes and besides this is not written as a technical book on gymnastics.

On each of the items of apparatus, there are four judges with a superior judge, known as the Head Judge. Male adjudicators preside over the men, and women over the women's events. A new post has been created to officiate at women's events, namely that of the Scientific Technical Collaborator (STC) who assists the Head Judge by recording every movement of each routine or exercise. In addition to the panel of judges,

Good form being shown by Boris Shakhlin while performing a vault to catch on the high bar at the 1966 World Championships.

A gymnast at a major competition enduring a last-minute stitching session.

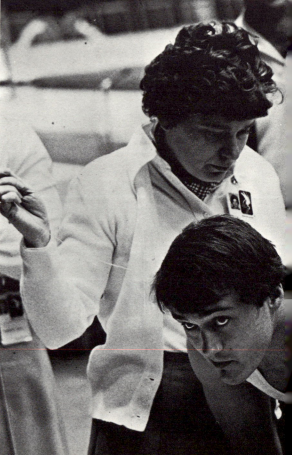

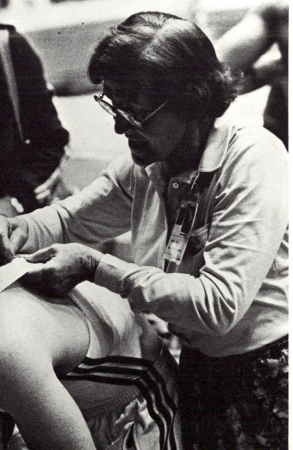

A most distorted view of the American, Kurt Thomas, competing in London in April '78.

there are assistants responsible for timing, and line-watching on the floor exercise. In Competition 3 there are two Head Judges on the panel to evaluate the exercises.

The highest and lowest scores from the four panel members are discarded and the two remaining ones averaged to obtain the final mark. Problems arise when the disparity between the scores awarded by judges is greater than the permitted levels laid down by the Code of Points. These figures vary according to the Competitions, but in 2 and 3, the differences must not exceed 0.10 for scores between 9.5-10.00, 0.2 for scores between 9.00-9.45, and 0.30 points for all other scores. When the difference between the marks is very great, the Head Judge will call a conference of the panel in order to try and determine the reasons for the variations in the scoring and settle them amicably. Only the Head Judge can contact the Jury, should it in fact prove necessary to remove a judge or coach from the competition hall, or in the case of a deduction from the score having to be made for the incorrect attire of a team or team member.

At the major internationals, the Jury is composed of the President of the Women's Technical Committee, a representative of the Executive Committee of the FIG, two other senior members of the Women's Technical Committee, and the Head Judge of the particular piece of apparatus over which the dispute has occurred.

The composition of the judging panels has been under close scrutiny recently, because of previous suspicions about the rigging of some results in major events. Under the new regulations, the judges are chosen just before the competition begins, in the hope that this will prevent the sort of aligned nationalistic judging seen in the past. However, this only partly solves the problem for, if some sort of bargaining is still to be effective, (and only those powerful gymnastics countries can afford to do this) there merely has to be a wider canvass of the respective judges' federations. There can be little doubt that the overall situation with regard to judging has improved with the introduction of new technical regulations, and the new Codes of Points. Theoretically at least, the sort of farce seen at Prague in 1977 should not re-occur under the new Code, however, the behind-the-scenes machinations, inevitably make such a prediction risky.

8 Gymnastics' Super Powers

Since its debut in the Helsinki Olympic Games of 1952, the Soviet Union has come to dominate the sport of gymnastics to an unprecedented degree. It was a bitter pill for the Finnish spectators to swallow to witness their wartime enemy take the medals from their own team, the previous Olympic victors, especially as the host nation for the Games. However, no spectator at Helsinki would have begrudged the Russians their medals because theirs was a stylish debut, combining dazzling artistry with some radically new techniques. Their assault on the men's titles was led primarily by Victor Chukarin, whose personal tally was three gold and two silver medals plus a 'share' in the Team gold medal. In the women's exercises, the Soviet team fared equally well. Led by Maria Gorokhovskaya, who won the individual overall gold medal, the women took the team gold by a little over six points from the Hungarians.

By the time of the 1956 Olympic Games, the Soviet women's team, led by Laryssa Latynina, was very much in the driving seat of world gymnastics. Interestingly for the Russian men, Japan, destined to become their greatest opponent in future competitions, featured well in the medal tables. However, with gymnasts like Azarian, Shakhlin, Titov, and Chukarin, the Soviets again affirmed their leadership in the team and individual events. The 1958 World Championships saw the last Soviet team victory over the Japanese men in World or Olympic events until the 1979 World Championships in Fort Worth, while only the Czechs in 1966 and the Romanians in 1979 managed to wrest the team title away

from the Soviet women in World or Olympic championships. The Soviet Gymnastics Federation has been the recipient of an embarassment of international victories since 1952, and with Yuri Titov spearheading their efforts from an official's seat, there is little doubt that they will seek to maintain their dominance by whatever means are at their disposal. The Soviet government takes great pride in the success of its gymnasts, viewing each victory as a triumph for its socio-political system. But, in the end, nothing can detract from the profound and most valuable contribution that Russia has made to the sport.

The Soviet success has been founded on a seemingly inexhaustable well of talent. Recognizing and making a commitment to developing potential at its most embryonic stage, is a skill which has proved the mainstay of Soviet gymnastics. With such a huge population it is no surprise that new talent is never in short supply, or that proper management of the sport demands a vast and complex machinery. Even within its own borders, political considerations play a role in the running of this machinery, under the aegis of the Soviet Gymnastics Federation. Politically, the USSR is an homogenous melting pot of different nationalities and cultures, more than a hundred in all, many of whose desires to fall into line with the Russification schemes of central government are strictly lukewarm. The dispensation of resources, financial and otherwise, is a convenient weapon with which to bring errant societies to heel, and the Federation tends to reward communities loyal to the Soviet by backing the aspirations of its youth

One of the finest and most popular of Japan's great gymnasts, Mitsuo Tsukahara.

91

while ignoring the areas of little political or economic importance or that harbor a dissenting population.

Undoubtedly, the system works, with almost automation efficiency. There are some three thousand gymnasia throughout the Soviet Union, boasting about four thousand six hundred formally qualified coaches. The specialist sports schools tend to have the best facilities and coaches, and competition for every coveted place in them is fierce. The competitive aspect of gymnastics is impressed on pupils from the outset, as strongly as the routine requirements of disciplined training, which accounts for the impeccable psychological preparedness of Soviet gymnasts, both as a team and as individual competitors, at all major events.

The fields of sports, statistical studies, psychology and medicine are of paramount concern to the Soviet training system, and absorb a larger proportion of its total sports budget than in any non-Iron Curtain country, the States included. In that fact is contained much of the secret of the amazing *consistency* of the Russians and other Eastern Bloc teams in their performances and the fulfilment of their expectations. So much data has been amassed and analysed that performance predictions for each gymnast can be accurately calculated, and training programs modified accordingly. The Physical Culture Institute is the umbrella organization responsible for this continual research and for putting its results into practise. The performance of all gymnasts are strictly monitored at every level of the sport.

Following the impetus generated by Olga Korbut and Ludmilla Turischeva, the Soviet Gymnastics Federation has continued to view the sport as a prime tool for fostering international respect and goodwill. Their current élite squad is as formidable as ever, geared to maintaining its dominance in a gymnastics future which promises to be more fiercely competitive than ever. Forming a strong team are likely to be Detiatin, Markelov, Azarian, Tkachev, and Makuts. Over the next few years the women's team can count on many equally illustrious names, such as Mukhina, Mostepanova, Filatova, Shaposhnikova, Davydova, Naimushina, Agapova, Arzshannikova, Yurchenko, Zakharova, and for a little while longer, the redoubtable Nelli Kim.

The Russians are aware that their pre-eminence in world gymnastics is currently under more serious threat than ever before,

Above:
Many a girl's heart-throb, Alexandre Detiatin of the USSR, at the annual Soviet display in London.

Left:
An unusual view of Yukio Endo, one of Japan's finest sportsmen.

pared and conditioned in the world. In fact, the DDR leads the world in its research into bio-mechanics and the application of medical science to sports. There are nearly seven hundred gymnasia throughout the country; every major athletics prospect is rigorously monitored, both by the administration at his sports center and by referral to Berlin (seat of the co-ordinating body for all this intensive research, called the Commission for High Performance Sports) virtually from cradle to grave. There, data returned from every sports facility in the country is carefully collated and analyzed, and instructions formulated to make any necessary amendments to training programs, individual regimes, and in matters of general sports policy. The superb computer and data-processing system devised for Leipzig University is at the service of the Commission for High Performance Sports, as are the University's team of programers and analysts.

As a result of recent defections to the West by certain East German swimmers and athletes, we have become able to construct a fairly precise picture of the kind of training methods that they were obliged to endure. To most of us in the free world, these seem extreme, even unethical and one must suspect that similar measures are adopted in the field of gymnastics education. The area of greatest public speculation and controversy is that relating to the systematic administration of drugs, many of which are prescribed by international sports bodies. This subject will be dealt with in a later chapter.

The names most remembered from the DDR men's team performances must be Koste, Barthel, Bruckner, and Thune. However, the East German Gymnastics Federation refuses to acknowledge the accomplishments of Wolfgang Thune, because he has recently defected to West Germany and has quickly become an Orwellian non-person in his former country. His arrival in the West has proved a fortuitous opportunity to achieve a greater understanding of the methods employed by his former compatriots. The East German women's names perhaps are more immediately familiar; Karin Janz and Erika Zuchold have both achieved widespread recognition. And who could forget the grace and charm of the delightful Angelika Hellmann? Steffi Kraker, Katharina Rensch, Silvia Hindorff, and Maxi Gnauck are among the most prominent young women gymnasts continuing

though they are unlikely to throw in the towel without a fight. Given the power they wield in the backrooms of the sport, it will remain to be seen whether the tussle for supremacy is restricted to the floor of competition auditoria, or whether incidents like those at the Prague European Championships will gradually reduce the sport to a shabby spectacle.

Where the Soviet Union leads, the East Germans seemed destined to follow. But before long, hopefully, the East German Gymnastics Federation may dare to permit some of its finest competitors to beat the Russians in a major competition. *Permit?* To the uninitiated, it appears that East German teams simply lack the confidence to beat the Russians in either the men's or the women's event. However, close examination reveals East German gymnasts for what they truly are, perhaps the best pre-

the traditions of their illustrious East German predecessors. There is little doubt that the team medals won consistently by East Germany in the past will become less securely that country's preserve in the years ahead, but it has the determination and the ability to keep producing exponents of the highest caliber in each of the disciplines.

Their ethnic, if not ideological, brethren across the Iron Curtain have for some time provided the most consistent and promising competitors in Western Europe. The facilities at the disposal of West German gymnasts do not, as yet, match those available on the other side of the Wall, but the number of well-equipped gymnasia and sports centers is increasing all the time and the general standard of West German gymnas-

tics is improving rapidly. The men have proven the more successful to date and one man in particular, Eberhard Gienger, has energized gymnastics in his country. He has dominated the scene for some years, his first major international success being a gold medal on the high bar in the 1973 European Championships. It is difficult to imagine from where his replacement on the national team will materialize. The recent defector, Wolfgang Thune, is a strong candidate now that he is available for selection to his new national squad, but his transition to a freer life has not been without its difficulties. Volker Rohrwick and Edgar Jorek are also in contention for team places. The West German women have not been very prominent in the international honors roll,

Above:
The enigmatic Russian star, Natalia Shaposhnikova, in the first flight phase of her vault.

Right:
Akinori Nakayama showing the sort of form that for many years made the Japanese men invincible in international competitions.

The embarassment of riches that the Soviet Union enjoys in its gymnasts means that someone like Paata Shamugia seldom represents Russia in top competition, although a man of his ability would make the national team in almost any other country.

their solitary success to date being that of Utta Schorn in the vault during the 1973 European Championships. Team success seems a long way off for both the men and women gymnasts of West Germany, the only medals likely to come their way in the foreseeable future being the result of individual flair.

A comparison of the fortunes of the two German states in the field of gymnastics is an interesting exercise because they represent test-tube examples of the differing social and sports attitudes that distinguish East and West.

When we think about that other great gymnastics nation, Japan, our thoughts revolve almost entirely around the men's events. For many years the Japanese men's team enjoyed an unassailable supremacy, taking every World and Olympic championship for twenty years from 1960. Finally in 1980, after many years of patient planning, the Soviet men managed to humble the mighty Japanese.

To the Japanese, the mental and physical discipline and awareness that is so much the essence of gymnastics is a natural extension of their traditional practices of Kendo, Judo, and Karate. Tradition plays a great part in every aspect of Japanese life and they consider gymnastics to embody all the traditional values that they hold in such esteem. It is the reason for the superiority of the men in the sport, for it has only recently become socially acceptable for women to indulge in competitive sports activities.

The two most famous Japanese competitors have already been mentioned in a previous chapter, namely Haruhiro Yamashita and Mitsuo Tsukahara. The vaults that bear their names stand witness to their inventiveness and supreme ability. Tsukahara was the most accomplished of the two, as his Olympic performance serves to underline. He won a gold and a bronze medal at the Munich Olympics in 1972, a gold, a silver and a bronze at Montreal in 1976. On both occasions, the Japanese team pipped the Russians for team gold. As great as these two men were, one of their teammates was arguably an even finer gymnast.

Sawao Kato won the combined exercises gold medal in two successive Olympics, in Mexico, 1968 and in Munich. He narrowly missed the gold at Montreal, where it took a superb performance by his Russian rival Nikolai Andrianov to deny him. His silver medal in his last Olympic competition was still a magnificent achievement. He was accompanied at Montreal by some very able teammates in the form of Nakayama, Kenmotsu, Kasamatsu, Tsukahara, and Kajiyama, but the best of the Japanese gymnasts formed an ageing team. The inevitable retirements soon opened up gaps in the team and it became apparent that there is not enough depth in the Japanese system to ensure continuity of success. A decline in their former high standards resulted in Japan's demise as a world leader at the World Championships at Fort Worth in 1980. The recent Collegiate Championships demonstrated that it will be some years before Japan can expect to assemble a men's team to regain the glories of the '60s and '70s.

Japan's women have never been able to complement the achievements of its men in international competition. Their only noteworthy success came in the 1966 World Championships when Ikeda won a silver medal for her exercise on the asymmetric bars. She and Mitsukuri also picked up a bronze each, Ikeda for the combined exercises. The Japanese women had never previously achieved a silver medal at any top level international competition, their only

other achievements being bronzes in the 1958 and 1962 World Championships. Now that gymnastics has gained greater popularity with girls in Japan, we can expect to see a rapid rise in their standards and expectations. It is probable that the competition that China, newly returned to the international athletics fold, will provide, will act as a spur to the efforts of the Japanese Gymnastics Federation in developing the talent it has at its disposal.

Funding of gymnastics in Japan relies heavily on media contracts covering the major events. The one most widely recognized is the prestigious Chunichi Cup, and this single event is the source of a major slice of the Federation's income. In this respect Japan is leading the way in demonstrating how the involvement of the media, especially television, can assist the growth in popularity and finance of the sport.

Shigeru Kasamatsu of Japan showing good form on the rings.

9 New Champions for the 80s

Nadia exhibiting perfect artistry on the beam. When top performers work on this apparatus, it seems to take on the width of a sidewalk.

The seventies started very securely for the Russians and in the area of women's gymnastics, there seemed no obvious threat to their continued superiority. It would take something very special to dislodge them and there seemed to be no rivals on the horizon to worry them. The year 1975 was to change all that.

Romania was the country that was to confound all the experts and alter the dynamics of the sport as profoundly as the Russians had done when they entered the international movement. Romania had been one of those countries that had enjoyed moments of success without ever really achieving the status of a major power. Its women's team had certainly eclipsed the men in terms of competitive prowess. It snatched team bronze medals in the 1956 and 1960 Olympic Games and the 1958 World Championships. Elena Leustean was Romania's most accomplished gymnast of the period. The next occasion when Romania featured significantly was the 1973 European Championships, where the talents of Alina Goreac and Anca Grigoras netted a silver and three bronze medals between them. Still, the men failed to set the international stage alight, though in the 1974 World Championships they gained respectability through Dan Grecu, who was awarded a joint gold with Andrianov for the rings exercise. Few people outside Romania were aware at the time of the intensive development program that had been instituted by the Federation of Romanian Gymnastics, and the fruit it was about to bear.

The world was alerted to the 'Romanian phenomenon' in London in April 1975 at the 'Champions All' competition. The revelation came in the form of a thirteen-year-old girl called Nadia Comaneci, whose performance stunned both the audience and fellow gymnasts with its technical content and virtuosity. The immediate reaction of the gymnastics fraternity was to dismiss this inspired debut as the one-off genius of an individual, rather than the product of a sophisticated gymnastics system. It was not long before the emergence of Teodora Ungureanu as a friendly yet close rival to Comaneci suggested that there was indeed a methodical system at work nurturing talent and producing potential champions. The 1975 European Championships served to underline this fact.

There are some 380 clubs affiliated to the Romanian Federation and these cover all forms of gymnastics, at every standard. There are less than 20,000 practising members of the Federation and from this pool some 4,000 regularly take part in competitions. The secret of the system's efficiency lies as much in its empathetic selection of potential gymnasts as in their subsequent training. According to Maria Simionescu, who played a major part in the formation of the new Romanian system, certain precise qualities are looked for in the young hopefuls seeking the system's support for a crack at a place in a future national team: suppleness, mobility of the lower back, natural speed, excellent balance, courage, intelligence, self-discipline, and morality. In addition to this fascinating combination of attributes, many years of highly specialized medical research into athletics and allied

Video equipment has been in use in Romanian training schools for some years now.

she may be enrolled at a sports school (an élitist institution for the exceptionally gifted) or join a club which will enable them to pursue their interest outside school hours.

Nadia Comaneci is a shining example of the results of this approach to discovery and development. It was decided that Nadia's home town would be the site of the first specialized academy of gymnastic science; a now famous school was founded in Gheorghe Gheorghiu-Dej, which was to provide for the education, academic and gymnastic, of the nation's brightest prospects for the future. The administrative and training team that established Gheorghe Gheorghiu-Dej has since moved on to set up a second major center in Deva, the home town of the coaches. The team that wrested the world title from the Soviet Union in Fort Worth was trained in Deva. There are now several leading gymnastics training camps and sports schools in the country; as in other Communist countries, those attending sports schools are treated as any other full-time student, in their case majoring in sports, and they are financed accordingly. This arrangement has for years given rise to cries of 'Shamateurism', particularly from those nations who accord a much lower priority to success in the international sports arena. The debate as to which attitude is more in keeping with the ethos and Olympic ideals of sport is endless. History has demonstrated that the principles evinced by the 'father' of the modern Olympics, the French Baron de Coubertin, back in 1896 were always somewhat unrealistic. A nationalistic attitude to international competitive success has existed as long as international competitions, and few athletes have ever been content just to 'take part'.

In criticizing the level of central government support for sports that exists in Iron Curtain countries, in perpetuating the argument that this makes a sham of the amateur status of athletes produced in such environments, one must remember that the United States is not so far removed from these nations, philosophically if not practically. The American system of sports scholarships has been formulated with precisely the same aim: to place talented athletes in a position of financial independence to concentrate without diversion on the business of perfecting their skills with the aid of sophisticated training regimes.

fields has taught the Federation to have a high regard for bio-potential assessments made of candidates at an early stage. These assessments provide an uncannily reliable advance idea of the way a gymnast's body is likely to develop. Although this firmly scientific approach and its application is far from being exclusively Romanian (the East Germans and the Russians do much the same thing), the Romanians seem better able to temper it with a natural eye and instinct for the gymnastic as opposed to purely physical potential of a young child. 'Talent spotters' visit the kindergartens and junior schools looking for aggressively playful children who can then be tested for any aptitude for the sport after which, if the coaches, teachers, and parents agree, he or

How often would one think that a bucket can be used to produce a champion of the pommelled horse? Yet here, in one of the 'secret' Romanian training camps, this humble device is put to exactly such a purpose.

In recent years Nadia Comaneci, a fourteen and a half year old schoolgirl at the height of her success, has been synonymous with Romanian gymnastics. Apart from creating Olympic history as the youngest ever gold medallist, she has received the previously unattainable 'perfect' score on no less than seven occasions, helping, incidentally, to spur the Russian, Nelli Kim, to a similar achievement on two occasions. Since then, Nadia has accomplished a unique triple, taking the European title in three consecutive championships — 1975, '77, and '79. It is a measure of the depth of talent that has been developed recently in the Romanian senior team that it was able to take the World team crown from the Russians without the services of its star performer, who had to retire with an injured wrist.

The men have tended to rely heavily on their most experienced and successful competitor, Dan Grecu, but there are now some fine up-and-coming gymnasts in the pipeline to succeed him. Checiches, Szilier, Cepoi, and Georgescu are all talented individuals capable of holding their own in major competition. The current overabundance of talent on the women's side has tended to mean that masterful athletes like Eberle, Turner, Ruhn, Chis, Vladarau, Dunca, Grigoras, Neacsu and Itu have been overshadowed by Comaneci. Ecaterina Szabo is a young girl with a promising future. Given its limited financial resources and population, the Romanian success story is a remarkable one, serving as an excellent example to many other sporting nations, large and small, of the rewards of application, determination and a resourceful approach to realizing

The Romanian Open
Championships provided
a graphic illustration of
the fallibility of
equipment when the
rings snapped.

ambitions. Maybe the country's very small-ness is a positive factor in its quest for championship titles. Its Gymnastics Federation tends to be less monolithic an institution than its counterpart in other countries, more in tune with developments in the sport and the needs of the athletes under its wing.

The United States has taken a long time to begin realizing its potential as a leading gymnastics nation. And its potential is enormous, with a population of a size that could virtually guarantee an inexhaustable supply of new talent, and as aggressive an attitude to sports success as any. However a land mass the size of the United States is not without its problems, particularly in organizing international representation in team sports, which may account for the fact that the US tends to shine in sports demanding virtuosity rather than team effort. As the Soviet Union has discovered, administering any organization on so vast a scale is a daunting task. Friction almost inevitably develops between the various regions, bodies and sub-committees making up the whole, as often by omission as by malice. A classic example of these inherent difficulties is the farcical situation that has existed in professional boxing for some years, since the sport's two American-based governing bodies failed to see eye to eye. The result is a roster of dual champions at every single weight, title fights that are recognized by one body but not the other and a general confusion that is seriously undermining the sport.

The United States Gymnastics Federation was founded at the end of 1962 and acknowledged as the sole representative for amateur gymnastics in the USA on its admittance to the FIG (International Gymnastics Federation), in October 1970.

There are fourteen member bodies represented by the USGF. These include organizations like the Amateur Athletic Union, the US Association of Independent Gymnastic Clubs, the Young Men's Christian Association, the National Gymnastics Judges Association, the American Alliance for Health, Physical Education and Recreation, and so forth. The enthusiasm generated by Olga Korbut has pushed the number of American gymnasts regularly involved in some kind of competitive program from about sixty thousand to around four hundred thousand, and the total number of registered gymnasts to around five million. This eruption of interest has imposed an enormous strain on the Federation, which

is serving the sport well in the circumstances. National training programs for the senior squads are quite sophisticated and well designed. The national judges associations have striven to standardize what was once a most inconsistent aspect of the sport as administered in the States, and increasing participation in international competition has yielded valuable experience to American coaches, competitors and judges. Membership fees represent only a small proportion of the sport's income; the real money comes from media contracts in respect of major competitions and international displays. Gate receipts are becoming more significant as the sport's popularity grows. American equipment manufacturers play a major role in

This amazing contortionist is Nadia in one of the Romanian schools in Bucharest. She trained here with her great friend, Teodora Ungureanu before moving to Deva.

Almost unrecognizable as the young Olympic Champion from the Montreal Games, Nadia Comaneci looking every inch a woman at the 1978 Strasbourg World Championships. Her lack of preparation for this event was clearly demonstrated by her weight loss during the course of the event.

assisting the domestic development of the sport, financially as well as technologically.

America has not had much success at international level until recently. Cathy Rigby's silver at the 1970 World Championships for her beam work was an oasis of success in a desert of mediocrity for the States. Cathy went on to become a familiar face on television as a commentator covering all gymnastics events with an American interest. The only other significant American performance before the late 1970s was that of Peter Kormann, who won a bronze medal for his floor exercise at Montreal.

The world started to take serious note of

American gymnasts as a result of their fine showing at the 1978 World Championships in Strasbourg. In the men's competition, Kurt Thomas, who is regarded as the best American gymnast to date, finished a most creditable sixth in the overall rankings and in so doing, picked up the gold medal for his floor exercises. Bart Conner and Mike Wilson produced performances of great skill, giving cause for optimism about the future of men's gymnastics in the States; as far as the Americans are concerned, the future means tomorrow! The next World Championships in 1979, were held in Forth Worth, Texas. These were viewed by most competing

With Christina about to try the Comaneci somersault for the first time, Gheorghe, her coach, stands close so that no harm can come to her if she misses on the first attempt.

104

countries as qualifiers for the Moscow Olympics. The American men's team certainly did the host nation proud, for they came away from the competition with the country's first ever team medal, a bronze, finishing behind Japan and the Soviet Union. Individually, the men fared even better. Kurt Thomas took the combined exercises silver medal, a gold for both the floor and the high bar, and two additional silver medals for the pommelled horse and the parallel bars. Bart Conner struck gold for his work on the parallel bars and shared a bronze medal with Barthel of East Germany for the vault. Suddenly, the US had become the country to watch out for, especially to teams accustomed to considering medals their preserve.

The women's team finished in fifth position overall at Strasbourg in 1978, showing much promise. Kathy Johnson and Rhonda Schwandt proved the most consistent of the Americans, Kathy winning a much deserved bronze medal for her floor work. The sensation of the tournament was a mind-bending display of artistry from Marcia Fredericks on the asymmetric bars, which won her the gold medal. It was a superb exercise. Unfortunately, the women failed to keep pace with the progress of the men's team in the year between Strasbourg and Fort Worth. Their two leading ladies plagued by injury, the US failed to win a single women's medal in Texas. Rhonda Schwandt had to withdraw altogether, and Kathy Johnson was forced to pull her new routines and difficulties. Marcia Fredericks and Chris Canary failed to live up to their reputations. Only Suzie Kellems ameliorated this picture of gloom. It will be interesting to watch Tracee Talavera develop once she starts competing regularly. The women's technical committee needs to make a sharp reassessment of its training policies and development program if it is to nurture a team able to take on the best in the world.

All in all, the future of American gymnastics looks reasonably bright, particularly on the men's side and in terms of a surge of popular interest and awareness, and we can expect Canada to benefit from a healthy scene south of the border. The charge of enthusiasm it received from hosting the Olympics has caused the Government to increase its support of amateur sports across the board, with gymnastics being a major beneficiary. The Canadian Gymnastics Federation has some twenty thousand members and is financed in a similar way to the USGF. The two personalities that are best known and most respected among Canadian gymnasts are the men's champion, Philip Delesalle, and Karen Kelsall. They have spearheaded the growth of national interest in the sport. With increased financial support has come the opportunity for international exchanges and competitions and the experience being gained by the Canadians is put to use to refine its understanding and expertise in all facets of the sport. We can expect to see Canadian gymnasts pressing their neighboring rivals strongly in the near future.

If asked to nominate any one country that could have the most profound effect on the future of the sport, one would have to name China. The huge gymnastic potential of that country is almost impossible to conceive. The world has known for some time that the Chinese have an affinity for gymnastics and forms of acrobatics, for similar reasons of history, culture and tradition as their oriental rivals, Japan. Sadly, during the so-called 'Cultural Revolution' it proved impossible to find out what developments if any were happening in gymnastics in the People's Republic of China. The ans-

wer, it would now seem, is not many, for gymnastics as well as certain traditional dance forms were actively discouraged during much of that period of social upheaval. Gymnastics continued with occasional interuptions but more as a form of art and exercise, the competitive element being frowned upon. With the closing of China's border, the country quickly fell behind, unable to keep abreast of the new ideas and techniques emanating from foreign gymnastics organizations, and unable to give its gym-

Kurt Thomas showing why he became America's leading competitor.

nasts the necessary top-level competitive experience. The country maintained a fragmentary national program of gymnastics events, and it is from this meager base that China is rebuilding its senior squads for international events. Once exchanges between China and other countries were reinstituted, the Chinese Gymnastics Federation responded swiftly and with conviction. The good relationship between Romania and China proved of great assistance to the Chinese in providing the inspiration for a revitalized gymnastics scene. As a first priority, it began to host some international competitions which brought to China the twin benefits of eye-opening experience and foreign currency, both much needed. China has since begun to demonstrate to the world that it is a voracious consumer of experience, and an excellent pupil.

The world soon began to notice its women gymnasts, such as Wang Ping, Chu Cheng, Ma Wen-chu, Wen Jia, whose good humor, ability, and grace endeared them to audiences everywhere. Men like Li Yueh-chiu, Xu Zhong-xuan, Tsai Huan-tsung, Peng Ya-ping, and Tong Hei, have all made a not insignificant contribution to the sport by bringing to international events an infectious enthusiasm, enjoyment of gymnastics and spontaneity of performance long lacking in these days of high technology routines and high-pressure competitive demands. The performances of the Chinese competitors at the Gheorghe Moceanu Games in Bucharest in 1979 were exhilarating and full of innovative movements. At Fort Worth later that year, they once again demonstrated their enormous potential in some very novel routines. In the process one of the women, Ma Yan-hong, took the silver medal for her performance on the asymmetric bars. Few people in the gymnastics fraternity doubt that China now has the capability to completely dominate the sport within as little as four years, perhaps the biggest uncertainty being the degree to which Sino-Russian politics can affect its progress.

At any time in its history, competitive gymnastics has been a complex blend of major and minor powers. There are several secondary gymnastics nations which are always in contention for medals at international events. Czechoslovakia, with women of the caliber of Vera Cerna, Eva Mareckova, Radka Zemanova, and men like Jiri Tabak and Josef Konecny are a force to be reckoned with. Vera Cerna won the beam

gold medal at the 1979 World Championships and followed that by winning the Coca-Cola International in London a few days later. Hungary is another important gymnastics nation. Even when its most illustrious competitor and prolific gold medallist on the pommelled horse, Zoltan Magyar retires, Hungary has sufficient depth of talent to continue picking up individual medals at major internationals. Men with the flair of Kovacs, Donath, and Molnar always present a threat. Hungary's female gymnasts cannot be dismissed lightly either, and Eva Ovari is a world class athlete of great potential.

The Cuban men look to be a serious threat to the established order, demonstrating considerable virtuosity and amplitude in all their work. What they lack at the moment is consistency, but Enrique Bravo has shown much promise. The British, French, Spanish, Italians, and Scandinavians are all of similar standard and with the occasional individual exception, could be described as heading the sport's second division. Thanks to the boom in gymnastics interest of recent years, youngsters entering the sport are bringing with them an enthusiasm and sense of ambition second to none, but their Federations still lack the supportive facilities that are essential to develop new talent to the full. The French, Italians, and Scandinavians are providing more residential sports courses and training camps, and gymnastics is one of the sports that can expect to benefit from them. The Finns, too, are modernizing their approach to the sport, itching to recapture the halcyon days of the fifties and early sixties.

Gymnastics as a technical sport has advanced immeasurably in the last four to five years; with so much national pride tied up in team performances at the big internationals, coaches and vast back-up teams of trainers, physicians, technicians and scientists are under immense pressure to push the limits of physical performance even further and as quickly as possible. There are bio-mechanical limits to the amount of stress that the human frame can tolerate and there is a feeling that we are running dangerously close to these limits. Special forms of body conditioning are already in use in order to stretch the tolerance of human physiology and it is these that have given rise to much speculation, criticism and fear both within and outside the sports world.

Bart Conner, one of the new breed of Americans who have proved so successful lately.

10 The Scientists and Technicians Take Over ...or Do They?

Since the storm first blew up about the use of drugs generally in sports, many self-appointed guardians of the ethos and morality of sports have pointed accusingly at gymnastics. This must have caused many parents anxiety; if there is any truth in the speculation the international gymnastics community will have to take a firm grip on the problem. Perhaps more pointedly, the medical profession should examine its role in the drugs controversy and be held answerable for its part.

The sports of athletics and swimming have provided much of the ammunition for the anti-drug lobby both inside and outside the sports fraternity. When a competitor fails a dope-test at a major international and is subsequently disqualified from future competition, the incident becomes public knowledge and a major media event. Multiply the incident (and there have been instances of sports meetings that seem riddled with cases of drug abuse) and an event becomes a scandal, a symptom of an epidemic of reckless chemical stimulation to ensure superlative athletic performances.

What people fail to understand in their hurry to tar all sports with the same brush, is that what may improve performance in one sport is not necessarily beneficial in another. The mechanical and psychological requirements may be entirely different. The most valuable information about medical manipulation of sportsmen and women has come from defectors from Eastern Europe, where the application of medical science to athletic performance has been most advanced. Research in this field has been long-standing in the Eastern

Many years of dedicated training have gone into producing someone of the caliber of Andrianov.

bloc, and its results more securely guarded than military secrets. A Gordian tussle has developed between the world's leading opposing experts, the East German alchemists and the British dope-testers. According to the testimony of recent defectors, it would seem that the honors to date have fallen to the alchemists. For every advance in detection, there is a response from the scientists to evade it. The drugs most readily associated with sports are anabolics, specifically, anabolic steroids. Their use by strength and power athletes is widely recognized, though there remain misconceptions as to exactly why they are used and what their effects are.

What is an 'anabolic steroid'? The word anabolic refers to chemically created compounds in living matter. A steroid is a compound like cholesterol, ergosterol, adrenal hormones, sex hormones, bile acids, or any of the group of sterols. It is the androgenic, or male sex hormonal, qualities that prove most useful to those for whom muscular strength and a high work-rate are important. The effect of androgens is to increase the size of the muscles and the body's utilization of proteins. The highly complex interaction of cortisol, a constituent of cholesterol, with amino acids and glycogen is of enormous benefit to muscles subjected to an arduous work load, as in prolonged training sessions. The fluid balance of the body, the flow of oxygen rich blood to the muscles and the breakdown of glucose into energy, all help to prevent lactic acid forming and, coupled with a precisely controlled salt balance, enables exceptional and sustained muscular effort to be undertaken.

Anabolic drugs are banned in sports, not just because of the unnatural advantages that they give selected competitors, but also because they are hazardous compounds to use. Misuse of anabolic steroids can prove fatal in extreme cases, and readily produce unpleasant, sometimes permanent side-effects. To women it presents a real danger of masculinization. In normal medical practice anabolic steroids are administered under the strictest supervision, for example, to help a patient regain strength after a prolonged, debilitating illness. It seems scarcely credible that in some East European states, these substances are freely available over the counter. It should be remembered that in athletic terms, the use of anabolic steroids has two main functions. Those are to increase the size of the muscle tissue, and to assist in the speedy removal from the body, and the muscles in particular, of waste products.

Jaeger performing the somersault on the high bar at Varna in 1974.

Japanese Olympic Champion, Sawao Kato, showing mastery of the most feared of the men's apparatus, the pommelled horse, at a demonstration for TV in 1967.

While an unnatural increase in muscular bulk may be useful in some sports, like the strength field athletics events, weightlifting and grid-iron football, it would be downright counter-productive in gymnastics. Heavyweights do not do well in gymnastics, the power-to-weight ratio being most important and very much against them. Having said that, it has to be admitted that male gymnasts have taken, and still take, anabolic steroids, though their use is not widespread and tends to be occasional, as if the gymnasts concerned are experimenting with the drug, rather than systematic usage. They have been used in both the West and the East.

Unfortunately, the use of all drugs in sports is self-perpetuating (one might say, self-accelerating). The competitive instinct, the craving to succeed is so strong in today's top-level athlete that once he has crossed the bridge of personal morality in the matter of drug-taking, ethics soon melt away. Research into the problem of drug abuse has shown that the only concern of culprits, their one lingering *fear*, tends to be of detection and the consequent damage to their careers. The damage to health is of little consequence. The justification for this strange ethic is simple: the others take drugs, therefore to compete so must I. And it is precisely this distorted conviction that cries out for

113

Gymnastics seemed a more relaxed and happy sport in the days when this lady, Polina Astakhova, was competing.

a concerted, international effort to stamp out the problem. No gymnastics federation has ever sanctioned the use of artificial stimulants, but many in both East and West turn a blind eye.

Drugs present a rather special and abhorrent problem in the field of gymnastics. Because of the extreme youth of gymnasts within the mainstream of international competition (remember that Comaneci and Korbut were barely teenagers at the time of their greatest triumphs), today's top competitors and trainees are very much under the mesmeric influence of coaches, the imposing federation that backs them, or even their own ambitious parents. Yet when a gymnast flunks a dope-test it is he or she

who suffers, possibly by disqualification for life, not the coach, not the army of doctors, therapists, scientists and administrators behind the gymnast, and not the federation. There is no real attempt to investigate the background to the competitor's use of an illegal substance — the pressures, the encouragement or insistence from certain quarters that led to it — or, indeed, whether the competitor was even fully cognizant of the nature and illegal status of the substance. Perhaps the inference must be that an adult male gymnast is aware of the nature of tablets, powders or injections that form a regular part of his training program, but is a twelve-year-old girl able to judge whether she is being fed prohibited drugs rather than vitamins, as her coach and team doctor have assured her?

The penalty for failing a drug test is severe; quite possibly disqualification *for life*. A career shattered, perhaps, thanks to a moment's recklessness, perhaps thanks to the inducement of others. And the punishment doesn't end with disqualification. The humiliation that a national team suffers as a result of the disqualification of one of its members is repaid, by ostracism in liberal societies and by something rather more sinister behind the Iron Curtain.

There is provision for appeal against disqualification, which is as well because the whole business of drugs control — detection, deterrence, even the formulation of a coherent, universally accepted policy on the matter — is still in its rather erratic infancy, the panic reaction to scaremongering by sections of the press. Bearing in mind that there *are* legitimate medical grounds for taking steroids, present methods of policing are unreliable, and as likely to cause injustice as they are easy to evade.

Almost as great a contemporary concern

Yuri Titov towards the end of another routine on the bars.

in the field of sports relates to the treatment of young women and girls and the supposedly unethical ways that their physical performances are maintained through puberty. It has become an emotionally charged issue giving rise to wild and sensational speculation, talk of 'child farming' and the use of bizarre, maturity suppressing medical techniques. The present demands and style of gymnastics mean that a small, slender figure is a great asset to female competitors, and the temptation to use every method available to retard natural development is great.

The dazzling display by Nadia Comaneci at the Montreal Olympics meant that for some time she would be the focus of world attention. Her fall from grace, not to mention the asymmetric bars, in the 1978 World Championships caused much speculation. She was so much taller and heavier than when they last saw her that many commentators assumed that her body must have been cruelly tampered with during the peak of her career; so 'rapid' a change in her morphology had to be evidence of this. Having decided that Nadia had been physically manipulated, to them it seemed to follow that all successful girls with a similar build had to be undergoing similar treatment. The popular theory was that the Eastern Europeans, who were dominating the women's events at the time, were administering hormones to the girls in order to retard puberty by several years and also to prevent them, after puberty, from developing a fuller, feminine build.

Despite exhaustive research and investigation by the monitoring bodies in the sport no medical evidence whatsoever has come to light to give credence to such theories. Certain medical scientists, particularly in Britain, have turned their attentions to the growing problem of drug and medical abuse in sports, and have been instrumental in achieving a tightening up of controls, but careful analysis of the results of the dope tests have failed to detect any chemical means of manipulating female body development. What is not generally understood, however, is that the desired ends which are assumed to be drug induced — namely an apparent delay in puberty and the maintenance of a low body weight — can be achieved by less sophisticated, more natural means. We shall examine these later.

The retardation of puberty is an emotive phrase that conjures sinister pictures of hormonal or genetic engineering, with a callous disregard for the long-term gynaecological consequences. In the average girl, with a healthy body left to its own devices, the onset of puberty occurs at the age of about 12; with boys the age is about 14. A margin of three years either side of the norm is generally accepted as natural, though a child whose puberty is three years beyond the average age tends to suffer some anxiety, to feel a little abnormal and inferior. Late developers are not that uncommon. Even for a normal child leading what one might term a relatively stable, ordinary life there is, therefore, a six year bracket during which puberty is a natural occurrence. Today's top class female gymnast is hardly the kind of child whose lifestyle one could describe in this way.

There is a definite tendency among the recent crop of world class women gymnasts to experience puberty on the late side of the normal age bracket, nearer fourteen or fifteen than twelve. But heated discussion about ovulatory suppressants and hormone treatment is uninformed. In most cases such drastic measures are simply not necessary.

The natural mechanisms of the body will allow a star athlete to work him, or herself, to physically fine tolerances as a result of the interaction of two factors, a carefully controlled diet linked to a high work rate. It is an astonishingly simple regime, yet the metabolic and hormonal consequences are complex and profound. The whole system is geared to a magic number — six. The aim is to achieve a physiological state where the total fat content of the body is restricted to a maximum of six percent of total body weight. A high-protein diet linked to a very tough physical program of gymnastic effort will hone the body to a sharp competitive edge. When the body becomes conditioned to such extreme demands on its functions, it modifies its normal balance to allow maximum concentration on 'essential' demands to the detriment of 'non essential' or 'interuptive' functions. This phenomenon combining with an extraordinarily low six percent fat level produces a body that is abnormally resistant to demanding physical distractions such as pubertal change, or when puberty has been entered, menstruation. The scope that the body's natural chemistry provides for tampering with the inconvenience of puberty and the start of menstruation is not lost on the athletes

Feminine grace and beauty revealed through the superb choreography of Caslavska's floor work.

themselves. Although it is easiest to control and monitor these factors in the authoritarian, total sports environment in which the élite gymnasts of Eastern Europe train, the secrets of a diet and work rate regime are not exclusive to communist competitors. Many Western girls with willpower and dedication observe self-imposed regimes with these ends in mind.

We cannot yet claim with confidence that there are no long-term risks inherent in such fine tuning of the female body, although the physiological and bio-mechanical experts involved in these practises would have us believe that they are risk-free. We do know that when the metabolism is so wholly geared to tolerating great physical exertion, it is least able to resist infection; the slightest viral or bacteriological infiltration will encounter minimal resistance and can develop into a more serious malaise in an athlete than it might in an ordinary individual. Another potential by-product of a permanently diet-conscious lifestyle coupled with exposure to exceptional stress is anorexia nervosa, popularly termed Slimmer's Disease. In the rigidly controlled environment of an Iron Curtain country it is a relatively easy matter to ensure that this condition never sets in. But in the West, where an athlete is left much more to his or her own devices, it is imperative that coaches, parents, teammates and friends are alert to recognizing the symptoms of anorexia. Sufferers are extremely adept at hiding their illness, even from themselves. Because of the physical demands of a sports career, the condition would soon become apparent in a gymnast. Cases of anorexia in young female gymnasts are rare, but a few have been recorded.

The whole question of the use of drugs and artificial stimuli to improve performance is still the subject of debate, a confused and hypocritical policy on the part of the international sports community, and increasing alarm. In the United States recently there has been an outcry at the use of cocaine by sprinters, and amphetamines are the staple diet of many athletes, stimulating the central nervous system in open conflict with the rules and morals governing sports, if not society.

In gymnastics, it is the coach who is charged with the responsibility of guiding his pupil and the duty of honoring the immense trust placed in him. When the use of anabolic steroids is regulated by law and

Sergei Diamidov executing his famous turn.

the drugs available only on prescription, there has to exist a conspiracy between, at the very least, the coach and a doctor for these drugs to form a regular part of an athlete's training program. In the circumstances, it is only when the sports community as a whole makes up its mind to attack the problem in a unified and determined assault on the backroom promotion of drug abuse that real progress will be made in the struggle to stem the tide.

Parents can take comfort from the fact that gymnastics is still relatively unsullied by such practises. In the West at least, the sport takes it responsibilities to young enthusiasts seriously and, longer than most other sports, gymnastics has retained some feeling for its ethos and origins.

Stoian Deltchev, one of Bulgaria's finest gymnasts.

119

11 The Promise of Gymnastics

Gymnastics, then, has become one of the most competitive amateur sports, exerting enormous pressures on both participants and organizers alike. The pressure that has given most concern to those within and outside of the sport relates to the physical stress placed on the human body by the ever increasing technical complexity of the elements within the exercises that competitors must achieve in order to remain at the forefront. Fears about 'human engineering' are largely unfounded, but it cannot be denied that there is a growing intrusion of science into the sport. Science can serve sports, helping to create a better understanding of the human body's capabilities, and ensuring the safety of both the performer and the apparatus. However, the manipulation of athletes by medical technicians, using unethical or illegal means to raise performance-levels, is a worrying practice in competitive sports, and one which appears to be gaining momentum.

Mercifully, as has been shown, gymnastics is not one of the sports that suffers most acutely from this trend. There are abuses, but they remain the exception rather than the rule. The overall governing body, the International Gymnastics Federation, has outlawed these methods as has the worldwide sporting community. However most abuse occurs with the connivance or at least the tacit acquiescence of national bodies or officials within the sporting organizations. In a country where there is a strictly organized and regulated sporting environment, it has to be assumed that all such breaches of drugs control are planned, and by implication, approved of. Where the

control of individuals in the sports is less rigid, it is less likely that the appropriate national association is directly involved; the tendency here has been for experimentation and misuse by rogue coaches and competitors. A positive dope test should bar a candidate from further competition for life, but it must be admitted that this seldom happens, especially if a sportsman is caught in his own country. Until the international sports community dedicates itself wholeheartedly to stamping out medico-scientific stimulation of athletic performance, and to instituting a system of sanctions that effectively penalizes those condoning powers and officials behind the discredited competitors, it will simply tighten its grip on the outcome of international competitions, stifling individual skill and virtuosity.

Gymnastics is a sport divided into two communities, comprising gymnasts, coaches, and judges on the one hand, and the sport's administrators on the other. In Eastern Europe, the distinction hardly exists, because, as a matter of principle, the administration of gymnastics is placed in the hands of people with experience and an understanding of the sport: ex-competitors, coaches and judges. Thus, policy-making is the preserve of experts who have an affinity with the demands and requirements of the sport. The West tends to prefer professional administrators, who seldom see the inside of a gymnasium, and are better qualified to run a private industry rather than a competitive sport.

Just as in communist countries where sport comes under the aegis of state control, so Western nations are increasingly unable to separate sport from commerce. Recently, and quite suddenly, amateur sports have become big business. The involvement of gymnastics administrators in the promotion of tournaments, the negotiation of media contracts and concessions, has exposed them to conflicting interests and has given a few individuals excessive control over the sport's purse-strings. When these professional people work strictly according to their own monetary terms of reference, they obviously should not be in a position to dictate the development of the sporting lives of those within their organizations. However, some national gymnastics bodies are suffering, or have suffered, from serious internal stress over divisions of opinion and priority between the money-makers and the competitors.

The competitors have their own problems over finance, as was demonstrated earlier, and it is in this area that administrators have a crucial role to play. The preservation of

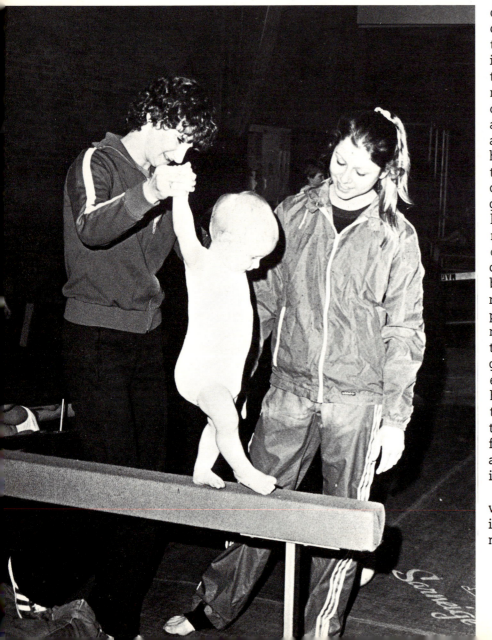

A future British champion? One year old Emma works out under the watchful eye of Yvonne Arnold, whose maternal support is backed up by the presence of Suzanne Dando, one of Britain's best gymnasts.

the athletes' amateur status is of paramount importance, as it is all too easy for a competitor to break the rules quite unwittingly. Receiving payment for competing at an event or taking part in a display is obviously not permissible as this deems the person a professional; however, the granting of expenses incurred in attending an event would seem an allowable re-imbursement to a competitor, but only on the assumption that the claims are entirely honest. Even in the case of valid expense claims, the finger of suspicion has merely to be pointed at an individual and he or she may find themselves suspended from competition until a long and painful investigation has been conducted and their innocence or guilt decided upon. In Great Britain, we have recently witnessed some extremely unpleasant scenes concerning fraudulent expenses allegedly cooked up between competitors and sponsors in the athletics community.

By ensuring that all expenses are paid directly to the national sporting body concerned, and that the competitors seek restitution from that body, the amateur status is not violated. Such a system is still open to abuse, but this time not by the sportsmen but by their administrators. The majority of these people are perfectly honorable, but there are always some rotten apples in the barrel. It does not follow, however, that the monetary manipulations that occur are for personal gain, for nowadays it is a frequent occurrence for some gymnastics bodies in the West to act more like investment brokers than sporting administrators. Thus, there have been examples of top gymnasts being awarded grants from certain recognized bodies and these awards being forwarded to their federation, and not being readily passed on to the appropriate individuals. These grants had been made in order to cover expenses which their federation could not meet and yet the gymnasts concerned had to fight hard to extract them. For if the federation could hold on to the money for a long enough time, interest could be earnt from it. While this may satisfy the accountants, it is hardly fair to the rightful beneficiary, and serves as a good example of the problem of marrying business ethics with sporting practices.

When unscrupulous administrators, motivated by personal greed and kudos, start interfering with the normal running of gymnastics, the effect is most divisive. These

A typical training session in almost any gymnasium.

people are normally those involved in selling the sport through publications, broadcasts, public competitions and displays. Ten years ago this was a difficult and demanding task, but since the mid-seventies, the demand for gymnastics has exceeded the supply in the West, so selling has become irrelevant; it is now all a matter of choosing the most favorable sponsor. Where the stakes are high, so are the favors, but if these are dispensed to the sport, rather than the negotiator of the contracts, we may overlook the ethical dilemma. Under the guise of protecting the amateur from being compromised by receiving expenses, for example in respect of an interview the media may wish to conduct with a gymnast, the administrator concerned will insist that all such matters must be referred to himself for approval, and negotiation. Ally this with censorial control over any official publications, allegedly necessary for good public relations, and suddenly one person has managed to stifle many of the democratic safeguards that can criticize abuses of the system. This undesirable situation has already occurred in one of the West European federations. There has also been a classic example of attempted interference in the rules of the FIG by a senior, non-sporting, official at a competition in England recently. He wanted orchestrated music to be permitted for one of the competitors 'because it would be popular with the audience', although its use was prohibited at that time under the existing Code of Points. The Head Judge correctly refused the demand but the unpleasant attitude of the official concerned soured the atmosphere of the event and, on return to her own country, the judge's own Federation were most displeased with the host country. The whole incident was entirely unnecessary, and as such represents a conflict between commercial and sporting priorities.

The implications behind this attempt to subvert the established rules are, however, quite serious and far reaching. Although it was known that the rule in question was going to be amended under the new Code, there could be no justification in flaunting the existing one. As already stated, the reason given was that it would be better received by the spectators if the orchestrated

tape was played. The idea that regulations should be changed according to spectator appeal, cheapens and degrades the sport. In fact, it ceases to be a sport and becomes a form of circus — mere showmanship.

Governments in the West tend not to view sport as a high-priority budget item and, in recent years, private sponsors have increasingly come to the financial rescue of amateur sports. They, through the events that they instigate and finance, provide a substantial portion of gymnastics' total income. However grateful the sport must be for this form of benefaction, however realistic it should be in recognizing that sponsors must themselves derive some benefit from their support, a stage is reached when dependence on commercial sponsorship is unhealthy. Now, more than ever, the time is right for even the most reluctant

Ludmilla Turischeva, in her new role as a coach with the Russian team, adjusting the distance between the bars during the European Championships in Prague.

Surely one of the most popular sportswomen, Nelli Kim, whose winning smile and Eurasian looks won admirers all over the world, many of whom had only a passing interest in the sport!

and the time to anticipate this need is now. An efficient sports complex has to be carefully and expertly planned. Gymnastics would be an obvious beneficiary of this enlightened attitude, being particularly suited to participation at every level of ability by the young people in inner-city areas, prone to the stresses of high-density urban living. Proper remedial gymnastics programs should be viewed as an important adjunct to a comprehensive health and welfare service.

Because of the physical and mental directness of gymnastics, it is a marvellous sport and pastime for developing self-awareness, and thereby, self-confidence. It not only builds a sound body, but is an excellent character former. It provides a competitive and disciplined environment in which young people can seek to express themselves.

What does a world class gymnast take with him or her from the sport on retirement? Probably a sideboard crammed with medals and cups, along with various small mementos from all the travels. Also lasting friendships, which span many national boundaries and political differences, and other man-made barriers to the free meeting of many peoples. Gymnastics is a pursuit which builds bridges between nations, rather than burns them, and brings people from all walks of life together in seeking a rewarding personal challenge. There may also be a few less wanted mementos such as the occasional stress fracture or scar, which serves to remind that person about the odd tendon or cartilage operation that may have proved necessary. Many who retire do not leave the sport, but plough back their experience and knowledge into it. It is they who form the backbone of the future of gymnastics.

All of us have a part to play in gymnastics. For the armchair viewer, the parent, participant, journalist or whoever, can all keep a vigilant eye on the way the sport evolves. In the end, it will only be able to take the wrong path if we tolerate it. It is arguably the most exhilarating and beautiful sport to watch, and the most demanding to participate in.

There are few more worthwhile endeavors that a child with athletic talent can aspire to than the discovery of self in a caring, disciplined, self-expressive, and competitive environment — which gymnastics, despite all, remains.

Western governments to invest in sports as part of a long-range social program. Social and industrial planners regard it as an inevitable by-product of the introduction of new technologies into industrial and commercial life that available leisure time will increase dramatically in the years ahead. The 'protestant work ethic' will have to be moderated within the course of the next generation, for a dangerous social vacuum will be created unless we are able to develop a new sense of community and purpose. Increased community sports and leisure facilities would be a part of the answer to the problem,

Glossary

A,B,C, parts or difficulties: Code for elements or combinations of basic, medium, and high or superior difficulty, and therefore value, respectively.

Amplitude: The greatest possible expression of movement.

Arab spring: A form of cartwheel in which the legs stay together from the vertical and there is a quarter turn before landing.

Artistic gymnastics: The six men's and four women's disciplines commonly associated with the Olympic Games.

Asymmetric bars: Used only by the women. Two parallel bars of differing heights, one at 2.3 meters and the other at 1.5 meters, both being variable by 10 centimeters either way. The supports for the bars are 70 cms. apart.

Back flip: A back handspring.

Balance beam: A wooden beam 10 cms. wide, 1.2 meters high, and 5 meters long.

Cartwheel: Sideways rotation of the body from feet, through invertion, to land on feet, using hand support at the inverted stage. It can be done without using the hands and is then referred to as an aerial cartwheel.

Code of Points: The judges' manual for gymnastics, produced by the FIG.

Compulsory exercises: Performed in Competition 1A and prescribed by the FIG.

Connections: The links between the various elements in a routine or exercise.

Croup: Section of the horse nearest to the vaulter, and on the pommelled horse, the section of the horse on the right of the competitor.

Crucifix: Performed on the rings, the gymnast holds his body vertically with his arms extended horizontally.

Dismount: The final movement of an exercise in which the gymnast descends from the apparatus.

Element: An individual movement from an exercise or combination.

FIG: Federation Internationale de Gymnastique, or International Gymnastics Federation, which is the governing body of the sport.

Flic-flac: The same as a Back flip.

Floor: Carpeted area of 12 square meters upon which the floor exercise is done.

Giant circle: On the high bar or asymmetric bars, a move in which the body swings through 360 degrees with the arms and body fully extended.

Handguards: Straps, normally of leather, which protect the palms of the hands from abrasion when on the bars, rings, or pommelled horse.

Handspring: A forward leap onto hands and then immediate thrust onto the feet, along the same direction of travel.

Handstand: Held position of the body on hand support with the body inverted.

Hecht: A vault or dismount in which the body reaches the horizontal, with the arms extended to the side, prior to landing.

High bar: The bar, made of metal, used by the men, at a height of 2.55 meters and width of 2.4 meters.

Hip circle: A complete circle executed with the hips against the bar.

Horizontal bar: See High bar.

Horse: Leather covered, rectangular structure of 1.60 meters in length and 1.20 meters and 1.35 meters high for women and men respectively. It is used in the vault.

Kip: Raising of the body from a hang to a support position.

Mount: Move that is used for the gymnast to get onto the apparatus in order to start the exercise.

Neck: furthest section of the horse from the vaulter, and to the left of the competitor on the pommelled horse.

Parallel bars: Item of men's apparatus which has two parallel bars of 3.50 meters in length at an identical height of 1.50 to 2.30 meters, being adjustable in order to accommodate competitors of different shapes. The width between the bars is also variable, being between 43 and 52 cms.

Pike: The body folding at the waist, and the legs straight.

Planche: A very strong move in which the body, using only hand support, is raised or lowered to the horizontal.

Pommelled horse: Horse, 1.60 meters long and 1.10 meters high on which are screwed two pommels, these being handles with a variable spacing for the gymnast to grasp.

Radochla: Named after its originator, a somersault between the asymmetric bars.

Reuther board: A popular form of springboard.

Rings: Men's apparatus of two rings suspended from a frame of 5.5 meters in height, the rings hanging about 2.55 meters above the floor level.

Round-off: See Arab spring.

ROV: Risk, Originality, Virtuosity. Factors which can earn bonus points.

Saddle: Central section of the pommelled horse.

Salto: A full somersault.

Scale: A held balance on a single leg.

Straddle: A movement with straight legs held wide apart.

Tsukahara: A vault named after its first exponent comprising a half-turn on and a one-and-a-half somersault off.

Tuck: Position of flight with the knees brought to the chest.

Uneven Parallel bars: See asymmetric bars.

Vault: Flight over or across the horse.

Voluntary exercise: Performed in Competitions 1B, 2 and 3. The elements and combinations are determined by the gymnasts.